1ˢᵗ *Space Renaissance International Congress - The Complete Acta, and the July 2012 Upgrade Resolution*

by Adriano V. Autino

A warm and special thanks to all of the SRI members, who participated to the congress, and contribute their time and resources to support humanity in the greatest challenge of all times: expanding our civilization outside the boundaries of our mother planet.

© 2012 Adriano V. Autino, Space Renaissance International
All rights reserved
ISBN: 978-1-300-20460-2

Title: "The First Space Renaissance International Congress – The complete Acta, and the July 2012 Upgrade Resolution"

Editor: Gail B. Leatherwood

On the cover: the Space Renaissance International logo

Please direct all enquiries to the author:

Adriano V. Autino
via Borgomasino 25/A
13040 Moncrivello (VC) Italia
email: adriano.autino@tdf.it

Chapter I The Issues presented to the Congress

Premises

The two Issues, presented to the congress by the SRI President, Adriano V. Autino, were intended to provide a summary of the Congress Theses[1].

The Final Resolution, presented to the congress by the SRI President, Adriano V. Autino, summarized the discussion held on the two Issues, integrating the main comments and suggestions raised during the Congress works.

The congress took place over 4 sessions:
- day 1 - June 25th 2011 - presentation and discussion of Issue I
- day 2 - June 26th 2011 - presentation and discussion of Issue II
- day 3 - July 9th 2011 - presentation and discussion of the Final Resolution
- day 4 - July 10th 2011 - election of the Executive Committee, approval of Financial Balance

The whole congress preceedings were held online, using the skype facility.

About 120 people subscribed to the Congress, directly attending or reading the transcripts of the sessions, made available on the SRI website[2]. A very larger number of people, in the order of thousands, were aware of the Congress, through the SRI Facebook site, and followed the works of the Congress by reading the Issues and the Acta published on the SRI website.

One year after the Congress, July 14th and 15th 2012, the SRI Executive Committee held a skype meeting, with the goal to review the Congress Final Resolution, to check the work in progress and adopt the needed corrections to the strategy. During such a meeting, the Executive approved the incorporation of the SRI US Chapter in Boulder, Colorado, to be led by Scott Van Brown, and decided some adjustments in priorities, in the frame of the 2011 – 2015 agenda.

ISSUE I – our philosophical understanding of the status of civilization and the SRI political program 2011 – 2015

"Assuring survival, employment and a future for all of our children by bootstrapping the Solar Civilization"

History of the Space Renaissance International

The Space Renaissance was conceived in June 2008 at the Convention titled *"Colonizing the Moon and the Near Earth Asteroids for a New Renaissance"*, held in Italy at Belgirate, lago Maggiore, by Technologies of the Frontier and Space Future.

The Space Renaissance Initiative was created online in late 2008 and developed during 2009. We issued several texts including a letter to G20 in London, 30 March 2009.

In 2010 the Space Renaissance Initiative incorporated the Space Renaissance International as an international association registered in Torino, Italy. The main goal decided by the assembly of the former SR Initiative was therefore achieved.

In 2011 we intended to hold a big congress in the US, but our organizational and financial powers were not enough. We therefore decided to hold an online congress, and to refocus our priorities from the huge program described in the book *"Three Theses for the Space Renaissance"* to a couple of projects, to be approved and kicked off during this congress.

Such projects will be the first step of our world-wide campaign targeted to gain a higher visibility and establish the Space Renaissance International in all the countries of Earth.

Strategy for space industrialization

Downsizing the cost to orbit is primary key

With reference to the great address given by Jeff Greason to ISDC 2011[3], a brief point on strategy is necessary.

For many years, even before the founding of SRI, the strategies of the main space agencies appeared to be:

- ESA strategy = mainly oriented to Earth (Earth observation, telecommunication, science); ESA never developed a space

human transportation vehicle (the Hermes space shuttle was cancelled in 1993)
- NASA strategy = science and exploration (one step ahead with respect to ESA, but not enough); after landing to the Moon, void of a long term vision and goals

We reaffirm our strategy as <u>space industrialization</u>. It doesn't mean to stop science and exploration. It means that priority shall be given – not just by the new space community and the space movement at large -- but by the whole space community (including agencies and traditional space industry) to space industrialization, starting from the Geo-Lunar space. The very first step on such a road-map is downsizing the cost to orbit. This could appear a tactical goal, but it is a very strategic one. If we do not state it clearly, any misleading concept could be still pursued, diverting public money and private investments from the very important goal: downsize the cost to orbit. Summarizing the SRI (near term) strategy:

- downsizing the cost to orbit (very preliminary urgent step)
- space industrialization (settling first in the Geo-Lunar system, begin living and working over there)
- conveying public support and private investments on the new space industry
- urging governments to develop Space Based Solar Power
- developing a space policy harmonizing the interests of the people of the Post-Industrial, New-Industrial, and Pre-Industrial countries

If we don't state point one, we could be viewed as supporters of the old space agencies policy.

If we don't state point two clearly, we could be viewed as just utopian and inconsequential space advocates.

If we don't state point three clearly, we will not really help the development of the space renaissance strategy.

Developing a strategy shared by all of the Earth's people: if we don't commit to point four, we may appear to focus on the needs and concerns of only a few of Earth's societies and ignore others.

Refocusing our commitment to astronautics, i.e. human space flight

The Methaphysics of Astronautics: 1950 – 1970

All of these Earthling Humans flew in space between 1950 and 1970: Yuri Gagarin, Alan Shepard, Gherman Titov, John Glenn, Andrian Nikolayev, Pavel Popovich, Valentina Tereshkova, Joe Walker, Vladimir Komarov, Konstantin Feoktistov, Boris Yegorov, Alexey Leonov, Gus Grissom, John W. Young, Gordon Cooper, Pete Conrad, Frank Borman, Jim Lovell, Walter Schirra, Thomas Stafford, Neil Armstrong, David Scott, John W. Young, Michael Collins, Vladimir Komarov, Bill Anders, Yevgeny Khrunov, Neil Armstrong, Buzz Aldrin.

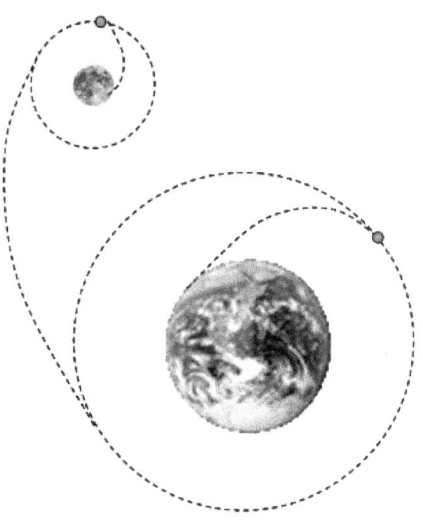

Just 20% of the world was industrialized, and the Earth human population in 1970 was around 3.7 billions.

The Space Ocean was still clean and pristine, nothing else that meteorites crossed the intrerface between Earth and Cosmos. The strategy and focus of the human space activities was Astronautics, though the main rationales were the cold war between the two main powers.

The Methaphysics of Astronautics: 1970 – 2000

During 30 years, from 1970 to 2000, Earth's orbit was "populated" by iron boxes, for Telecommunication and Earth Observation. The Moon was forgotten, and industrializion kept on growing up on only on the surface of our mother planet.

Earth human population in year 2000 reached 6 billions. A "cathedral in the desert" was deployed, the International Space Station: expensive, orbiting on an orbit useless to be used as an intermediate station, doing less more wrt what the MIR previous station already did.

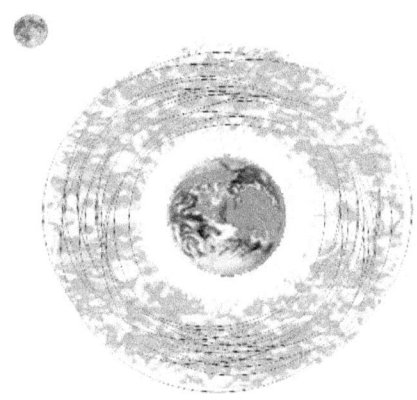

The Space Ocean near Earth was filled of garbage. We threated it not differently than the Earth Ocean: it is so big, we can throw all of our wastes overthere.

The strategy and focus of human space activities was: Earth & Business.

The estimated total mass of space debris is about 5,500 tons. A realistic view o the LEO space debris in the following picture (from Wikipedia).

The Methaphysics of Astronautics: 2000 – nowadays

During the last 10 years, Earth's orbit kept on being filled, by thousands of satellites for TV, Earth observation, scientific payloads.

Though many papers were written about space debris, none initiative was taken to begin a reclamation of the Earth's orbit.

The main space agencies are in deep crisis, and we don't know what to do with the Moon: many think to "populate" it with robots...

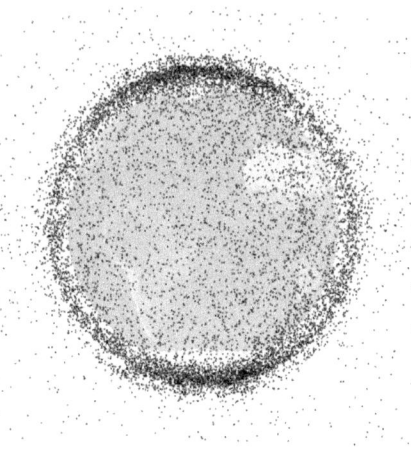

India, China and Brazil begun their industrialization, and rapidly aim to the first places, as economic powers.

Earth human population will pass 7 billions before the end of 2011, and the rate between births and deaths is 2,34. Fertlity is sadly declining in all the world areas, and Earth is closed in a cage of iron garbage.

The strategy and focus of the human space activities is caged by the interest of greedy lobbies: oil, weapons, banksters.

The Civilization is in the middle of a process we could call *"Methaphysical warming"*, a mix of:

- lack of resources and energy,
- people's rights demand,
- environmental decay,
- resource wars,
- growing population,
- global industrialization,
- fear of the future (waiting for the huge holocaust, or *armageddon*)

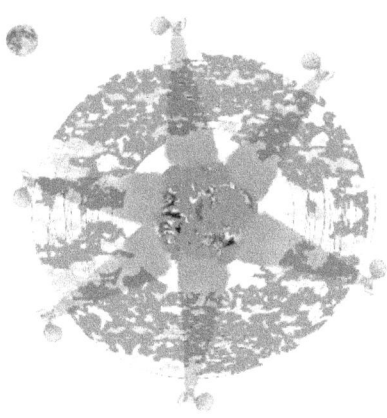

The Methaphysics of Astronautics: what do we need?

Do we need more energy and resources in order to continue our development (only) on Earth?

That would just accelerate the implosion of the civilization, and not to continue its development.

What we really need is to begin moving our development outside Earth, begin to use exo-resources for the space infrastructure building.

What we need is to finally **bootsrapping an exo-development**!

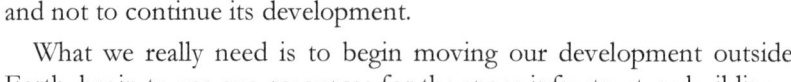

The Strategy of Astronautics

Our strategy comes from our methaphysics (i.e. perception of the world).

Our perceived world is the Solar System, and it extends to the surrounding Oort Cloud, made of trillions cometes, providing water and basic components of life in the whole Solar System (last info says that water was detected even on Mercury!), while Asteroids contain almost pure metals. Exo-water means exo-oxygen, and everything needed to support human life and other Earthling forms of life that will accompaign us in our expansion.

When we talk about environment we are not bounded to the environment of this planet: we can and shall take care of, and earn life supporting resources, from an environment 200,000 Astronomical Units diameter large!

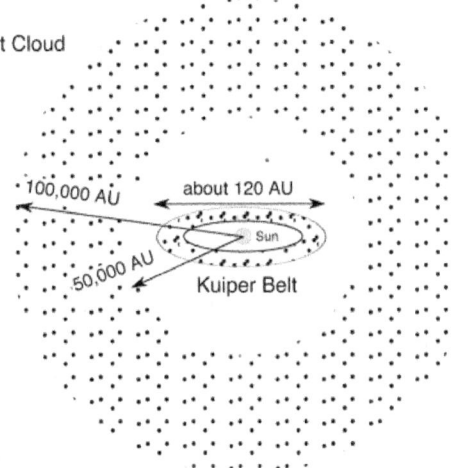

The Oort Cloud and Kuiper Belt (not to scale!). Extent of the two comet reservoirs are indicated. The nearest star is almost three times farther out than the Oort Cloud.

Our strategy, in the current critical age, shall be focused *to ignite the human exo-development*.

- downsize the cost to orbit (key to everything following)
- focus on Civilian Astronautics
- take care of the Earth's orbit, our interface to Cosmos
- master the orbit environment, that will be our greather home, in this century
- progressively use exo-resources, from Moon and NEA, to develop the Earth-Moon infrastructure

- use part of the Space Debris to build the Orbital Infrastructure
- develop SBSP firstly to feed space customers
- develop SBSP *following* Civilian Astronautics, *not before*, and *not instead* of Civilian Astronautics
- move more public money from military to civilian space activities
- support convey of investments into the new space industry

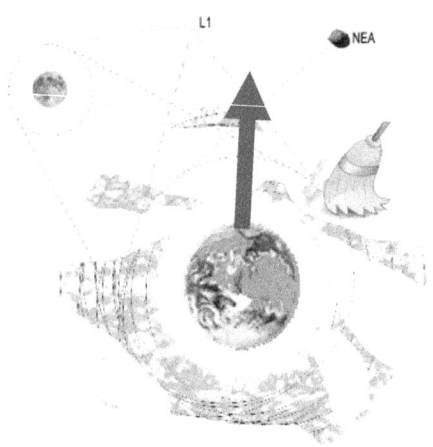

The status of civilization

As we wrote in our theses, the growing complexity in a closed environment leads to an unsustainable increase of pressure, as testified by all the social, economic, environmental, political indicators:.

As we wrote in some recent newsletters, the signs of what Stephen Hawking called "implosion of the civilization" are already visible, on a path of failures and disasters, both natural and caused by the human risk assessment immaturity.

The Chernobyl disaster represented the ideological bankruptcy of the Stalinist Soviet regime and its ideology. We are in total agreement with that interpretation. A low-quality ideology produces low-quality science. If this was and still remains true for the old-fashioned Soviet nuclear power plants, kept working in defiance of every principle of security of the population, it is certainly true for the Gulf of Mexico in 2010 and for Fukushima in 2011. Such two disasters represent the failure of the liberalist ideology.

The social movements triggered by the North African revolutions express a double awareness. First, people around the world ask for more democracy and an economic system allowing the reduction of inequality, while the current financial leadership is increasing inequality everywhere. Second, the so-called "Web 2.0" is revealing the social power of the *social* networks. That confirms the excellent intuition stated by Amartya Sen (Nobel prize for economics in 1998) that the spread of information is very much more effective than guns in spreading democracy in countries still subject to tyrannies.

A key problem of the *advanced world economy* today is the lack of new industries which are needed to replace the old industries shipped out to China, India and elsewhere. The popular demand for new industries will grow to large scale.

The new economic powers, China, India, Brazil, are experiencing a season of growth, and the people there are aimed by a strong hope of development and progress, to achieve the same wealth level of the post-industrial countries. But such aims already knew a serious standstill with the global crisis initiated in 2008 and not yet terminated. It appears obvious to anyone willing to see the reality, that the resources, energy sources and environmental capabilities of Earth are not enough to sustain the civil development of a seven billion civilization.

Nothing can solve the above problem except developing space travel and opening the space frontier. To date, however, both the governments and the world finance have refused to invest in this new frontier — to the amazing extent that, having walked on the Moon in 1969, Americans won't even be able to get to space later this year! The people of both the post-industrial and the new industrial countries have a strong interest to unify their efforts, in order to set the civilization on the right path: upward!

Summarizing, what our civilization desperately needs are the following items:

- more safety, to keep on developing the global economy
- new industries, to quickly replace the jobs lost in the global crisis, to avoid losing know-how and progress capabilities
- new resources, to allow the whole humanity to reach a better living condition, a full inclusive society and an enhanced ethics, without causing a collapse in a finite environment
- a true general cultural renaissance, that can be ignited only by the opening of the space frontier and the beginning of the human expansion into space

Such a process will be long and nothing is guaranteed, but of one thing we are quite sure: failing the opening of the space frontier there will be no future, and our civilization is condemned.

Failing any substantial improvement of the above conditions during the next 10 years, the scenario sketched by Stephen Hawking and James Lovelock -- human population falling to one billion or less during this century – will be very likely.

We perfectly know that one only true *lifeboat* exists, in this age: downsizing the cost to orbit, and launching the space economy revolution.

Having clearly presented all of the strategic middle and long term goals in our Philosophical Manifesto, the SRI indicates the following themes, as priority for the next four years: (i) space tourism – both suborbital and orbital; (ii) space based solar power; and (iii) Geo-Lunar region industrialization, as the three main leverages suitable to begin building the space industry, market and economy.

The new space industry and its business figure had an exciting growth, after the victory of X-Prize by Scaled Composites in 2004, from around 20 up to 100 companies and growing. But that could be still too weak to reverse the crisis and re-launch the economy in time to avoid a general bankruptcy. That's where the governments and public money keep having a key role, not only promoting space science and exploration, but also supporting the private industries in their dramatically decisive task of opening the Earth orbit to private enterprise!

The task of the SRI and of the whole space movement for the next 4 years is then clear and simple: we must quickly elevate the public awareness of the absolute urgency to open the space frontier.

The main general needs

The main general needs of the civilization can be summarized as follows.

Philosophy

a) all of the existing ideological wings are a residual of the past century, and there are no signs of new ideological concepts, compared to the challenges of this age

b) neither *utopian socialism* nor *utopian liberalism* exist in the real life; in real life we experience pitiful caricatures of utopias -- *real* socialism and *real* liberalism -- ideologies of such low quality that one wonders how we can repeatedly be so stupid and keep on voting for

Utopia, then accepting what a quite insufficient political personnel is dispensing to us in reality

c) the right wings – in different measures, due to different regional cultures, religious and ideological climates – are irresponsible, unscrupulous business oriented, Mafia like, and often blatantly immoral

d) the left wings – with due differences as seen above – are generally hegemonized by greenish nihilist ideologies, orphan of socialism, and often still aimed by obsolete class hatred

e) the best intellectual clubs – sadly including so far the Space Renaissance! – appear unable to escape endless discussions in which far distant science fiction items are mixed with feasible steps in the good direction

f) we, as SRI, could make the difference, and begin to finally make available a new ideological pole, oriented to the future, bearer of strong humanist values, only if we will be able to agree on a minimal shared agenda, and seriously start to move it into the society.

Energy

a) oil, coal and nuclear power, if developed at the scale needed by our seven billion civilization, pose a too high environmental risk, as demonstrated by recent and old events

b) the so called 'renewable' earthly energy sources, such as photovoltaic, wind, and other popular alternatives, are not economically competitive with the traditional sources; however they will not be quantitatively enough to support the industrial development needed by our seven billion humans civilization

c) some promising new energy sources have recently appeared, such as shale gas; that will be a low cost competitor of the renewable energies, but on the long distance it doesn't represent a true alternative, since it still keeps the whole thermal burden inside Earth atmosphere

d) the sole true alternative, on a long distance, is Space Based Solar Power, but we shall be realistic about SBSP

e) before SBSP can be economically interesting and competitive with other sources, the Earth-Moon infrastructure must be built and operative

f) we should be aware that the main market of SBSP will be space customers; only when that market is developed, will SBSP be competitive also on Earth
g) given the above situation, SBSP is currently an item for governmental initiatives, more than for small and medium private investors
h) we praise the Japanese government, the only country who is making a true effort on SBSP, planning to fly a demonstrator in 2020, and a production plant in 2030
i) we believe that the recent disaster of Fukushima should encourage Japan to an even bigger effort on that road
j) we solicit governments – and possibly consortia of energy industries which accumulated high profits with traditional energy sources -- to follow the Japanese example, and open orbiting yards to build space power plants.

Safe industrial and civil development

a) the global economy is starving new industries, to quickly replace the jobs lost in the global crisis, and avoid losing know-how and progress capabilities
b) several nihilist ideologies, dominant during the last 30 years, suggest that humans are a cancer, that people are useless, just 'mouths to feed', and that any technological effort will make the planet's situation worse
c) in such a philosophical decay, youths are left to their own, without jobs and without future, prey of mafia, superstition and anti-science irrational beliefs
d) the above represents an intolerable *cultural risk*, that is properly assessed only by a very few, numerically insufficient, people on Earth
e) given the intolerable risks of a continued industrial development on one only planet, and the desperate need of new industrial development, our civilization must begin to expand into the solar system, as soon as possible. We are already paying an incredible delay of 50 years
f) the global economic development is blocked by the dominant closed world pre-copernican philosophy, and is so far caged by the

most backward lobbies and bankers, still ruling among financial, oil and weapons sectors most of all

g) we state that the only new industry able to reverse the global crisis, and to create millions of jobs in a short time, is the new space industry that will develop the Geo-Lunar space industrialization, if duly financed and supported

h) we also state that people are resources, not problems, that the big number of humans is our true richness, and this will be proved when we expand into the solar system

A political agenda for next four years

a) <u>the SRI will give priority</u>, and call the whole space movement to give priority to, the following strategic development topics:

    a. downsizing the cost to orbit, using existing or near to existing technologies, concentrating investments and government support on the companies already working for such goal

    b. suborbital and orbital space tourism

    c. industrial development of the Moon and the Near Earth Asteroids

    d. space based solar power

b) <u>stimulate the growth of a new mass space industry</u> - choosing a few suppliers was the old method; today we need to stimulate the growth of a *new mass space industry*, oriented to the market (no longer to agencies), many small and medium enterprises, enthusiastic space entrepreneurs, not just old industries who were used to depending on the *captive market* of agencies.

c) <u>international space investment funds</u> - encourage the creation of *International Space Investment Funds*, where all citizens can invest their own money for the sole truly worthy industrial enterprise: space colonization. Encourage the creation of all possible facilities to allow the growth of the space funds, such as: 1% on credit cards, a small percentage on sport tickets, luxury goods, or anything can let people know what they are doing: donating small amounts of money for the future of our children!

d) <u>tax discounts and friendly financing</u> - such an emerging space industry should also be supported by public funds, to validate the new technologies for low cost and safe access to Earth's Orbit (remembering what Scaled Composites was able to accomplish in 2004 with just 30 million), giving tax discounts and financial help to all the small and medium enterprises that are developing technologies, systems and methodologies for astronautics.

e) <u>a wide international cooperation, for a peaceful space development</u> - all the world leaders both of already space faring Nations and Nations which aim to develop space activities, should run wide-scope international collaborations & initiatives for support and fostering a space based commerce & trade marketplace through joint projects and mutual support. In order to achieve such a goal, they should create and update an International Space-peace Treaty, for the peaceful development of space, and for banning of all weaponry development in outer space. For the US and other nations, to remove the political hurtles designed for preventing international collaboration and sharing of human collective intelligence in space exploration and development, such as the ITAR and similar rules.

f) <u>sustainable space exploration and industrialization</u> - in short, should we be courageous enough to implement the above outlined program, we will have a truly sustainable space exploration and space (industry & economic) development, and we will see millions of high-tech jobs (the jobs that are sustainable and have never before seen) to be created.

The program to ignite the Space Renaissance

The main SRI Projects

If the goals are clear, the means to achieve them are not as clear.

In our theses, we drafted a program based on seven steps:

Figure 1. The SRI Seven Steps Stragety

Though in our current condition it could appear a bit too ambitious, we should keep it in mind, since things could begin to run at a quite faster pace, if we would be able to move the right initial steps.

The registration campaign didn't give the hoped results, at least so far.

Therefore we shall anticipate step 2, work to enlarge our audience, and focus on the project as a leverage to get some grants by foundations which could estimate our initiative worth and useful, and some imporrant donations.

Having a budget, we will have the possibility to dedicate an amount of paid hours to develop the project.

The proposed projects – as will be detailed in Issue II – will be the following three:

- a) the Civilization Risk Assessment and Management (CRAM) Project
- b) identifying and defining the Best Strategic Space Business Development to ignite the Space Renaissance (BSSBD)
- c) Feasibility study and design of a virtual O'Neill habitat, to be settled at an earth-Moon Lagrange Libration Point

The SRI agenda from 2011 to 2015

In the same time, the 2011 registration campaign shall start vigorously and reach the objective of 10.000,00 €,

With this money, we will finally have the ability to purchase some newspaper advertising, and make our message exceed the boundaries of the space community, to reach the real society, and begin recruiting sincere humanists there.

Our agenda for the next 4 years is the following one:

Date	Development
July 2011	SRI Projects kick-off, 2011 registration campaign kick-off
January 2012	Media advertising campaign. Incorporating the SRI US chapter
June 2012	SRI Projects check 2012 registration campaign kick-off
January 2013	New media advertising campaign, with first data issued by the SRI Projects
June 2013	SRI Projects results evaluation, dissemination and decision about follow ups
January 2014	SRI Projects issues dissemination, development of children's projects
June 2014	"Medici Space Foundation" building first steps
January 2015	"Medici Space Foundation" project check
June 2015	SRI second congress "Medici Space Foundation" incorporation

A growth setup for Space Renaissance International

The growth of SRI, during the next four years, cannot be continued in a casual and random style, as it has been so far.

Assets

We shall establish few but sure assets:

a) a better management of our web facilities, and possibly the creation of a blog

b) election of a general secretary, who will coordinate our efforts at international layer

c) organized initiatives toward some selected organizations, foundations, or communities that could be our allies and share some of our goals

d) take care of the 90 organizations joined to the SRI, running active collaborations

e) a systematic action targeted to group together the many supporters of the SRI in all the countries, allowing the creation of chapters everywhere

f) a systematic action targeted to join the whole space movement in the Space Renaissance International, in order the space movement can speak with one only voice on some shared goals.

Alliances

Talking about possible alliances, we point out the following:

a) foundations, owner of humanist principles in their mission statement should be our 'targets', trying to establish joint projects or, as minimum, to get grants to support our projects

b) scientific foundations, available to support our projects

c) universities, the help of which we should solicit for our projects; in universities we could also get interns, to volunteer in our projects

d) sectors of opinion movements, such as some environmentalist tendencies, as can be found e,g, in the US, when they are not against the human development nor science and technology

When talking with environmentalist movements, we should always keep in mind that we are asking them to share some of our goals (we don't claim they will 'marry' the whole of our program, of course, though we will welcome all individuals who will subscribe to the SRI).

We always have to point out the philosophical differences, before trying to agree on some shared points.

Signing the main philosophical differences will make some of them to reflect and maybe acknowledge the anti-human characteristic of many green pre-copernican concepts, based on the closed world philosophy.

Never being sectarians, we shall bear in mind that this is our mission, to spread a post copernican vision of the world.

Issue II – Three Projects for the Space Renaissance

1) Civilization Risk Assesment & Management Project - Abstract
2) Detect the most promising space industrial development line - Abstract
3) Feasibility study and design of a virtual O'Neill habitat, to be settled at an earth-Moon Lagrange Libration Point – Abstract

General setup

The projects will represent the main commitment fo the SRI during the next four years, up to 2015. The key points of our road-map are the following ones:

a) a dedicated SRI task force will be created just after the congress

b) to draw the Statements Of Work and basic WBS of the projects

c) to seek grants from foundations; to do that we will have to draw a proper plan, identifying the foundations, to take contacts; we shall be prepared to better develop the ideas, provide business plans, fill questionnaires

d) <u>to involve universities and research centers</u>, from the very beginning; the SRI can gain visibility and achieve precious relationships in the academic world; the most suitable university faculties will be identified for each project, and a plan of contacts will be developed as well

e) <u>to seek sponsors and donors</u>, creating funds is a of big relevance, or the projects will never step ahead

f) <u>to contact celebrities</u>, proposing them to be testimonials and to give funds for the development of the projects

g) <u>to hold conferences everywhere</u>, to spread the word of the Space Renaissance, to invite people to support and collaborate; the SRI President is available to go; other speakers will be identiied as well.

On the background, we shall always have in mind our strategical goal: to create the basis for the Medici Space Renaissance Foundation, and the seed capital for the Space Investment Funds.

Projects

Civilization Risk Assesment & Management Project – Abstract (proposed by Adriano V. Autino)

Several philosophers, different for school and ideological orientation, wrote that the Civilization is running global fatal risks, during the 21st Century. The most famous two are Stephen Hawking and James Lovelock, but other ones, e.g. Paul Ziolo, made similar forecasts. Our unsustainable presence on this planet is now at 150% and heading to 200% by 2030 (World Wildlife Fund 2010 report). The development of the new industrial countries will accelerate such a process.

Our astronautic humanist analysis lead us to the basic concept that, keeping on growing up in a closed environment, the civilization will reach a breakpoint, after which it will rapidly start to decline in number, in culture and technology. That point can be defined as implosion or crash of the civilization.

But such forecasts, though very logical, are so far just intuitive.

When will such an event occur? How much is it probable?

And which risks are however impending, should the Civilization remain confined into the boundaries of the closed world philosopy? We can list a bunch of global risks:
a) the economical development will be stopped by scarsity of resources and energy
b) the global market will decrease, due to continuous crisis and shortage of raw materials and energetic resources
c) the regional conflicts and terrorism will increase in number and intensity, due to a continuous economic crisis, and the decrease of markets and jobs
d) the shortage of energy sources will lead to increase the risky activities, such as drilling deep underwater, building nuclear plants where the sysmic risk is high, increasing the use of coal and oil
e) the continued ise of oil and coal will worsen the environmental pollution, like acidification of the sea waters
f) keeping on throwing dangerous wastes into the sea will compromise the source of life on Earth, decreasing the fish resources, just when the increased world population would need it more
g) possible climate changes – be they warming or cooling, due to human industry or to natural changes like solar activity – will cause large destruction of lives and economy
h) a possible impact with a Near Earth Asteroid or a Cometoid could cancel the life on Earth in just a few days
i) last but not least, a global nuclear conflict, though less probable after the end of the cold war, could destroy our civilization as well
j) environmental crisis and famine could lead to vast number of people moving that results in conflict that could all too easily slide toward nuclear madness
k) generalized cultural lethargy, derived from loss of hope, could lead to the potential of mass suicide.

The above is an incomplete list of the global risks that our civilization is running, *today*, not in a distant future.

The SRI wants to develop the knowledge about the global risks, with the help of universities and research institutions, and setup a risk mitigation plan, to be submitted to all the Earthly governments. We aim to associate a world wide survey, asking people to give their feelings and impressions about global risks, possible countermeasures, their availability to support such countermeasures and to exercise pressure on governments, for a policy more oriented to human safety and to the future.

Detect the most promising space industrial development line – Abstract (proposed by Alberto Cavallo)

In the SRI forums, many of our members discussed several ideas, trying to identify the best catalyst of the Space Renaissance. Some of us supported Space Tourism, some others SBSP, Moon Industrialization, Orbital Industries, NEA Mining, Oribiting Debris recover and partial reuse, to build the Geo-Lunar Sytem Infrastructure, and others. The SRI is strongly aimed to support the best "champion" industrial activity, who can raise huge capitals on the market in few years (both by investments and by selling new space services), and self-sustain the enhancement of astroanutic technologies.

All the discussions were animated by passion and good will, but we need more. We need a scientifical assessment, based on figures, statistics and trends. We will propose this project as well to universities and research centers.

The most promising solutions should be investigated and compared, in order to define a strategy for the industrial development of space.

Let us resume a first list of business activities in space considered to be used to bootstrap the process:
- space tourism
- space based solar power
- Moon and near Earth objects mining/settling of transformation industries for:
    - rare elements
    - construction materials
    - propellants
    - water
    - etc.
- orbital debris recovery
- etc.

For the most promising activities the preliminary business case shall be studied:
- market analysis
- technological needs
- capital costs including investments in research, if needed
- operational costs
- time schedule

This could be done with the cooperation of the academic world (universities, business schools, polytechnic institutes).

Feasibility study and virtual mockup of an O'Neill habitat, to be settled at an earth-Moon Lagrange Libration Point – Abstract (proposed by Kim Peart)

There are some threasures more or less unused, if not forgotten: these are the works of Gerard K O'Neill during '70s, Krafft A. Ehricke in the same period, Werner Von Braun and others.

They are not forgotten, because we at SRI, and many other space advocates never will forget our beloved Maestros.

The SRI aims to retake the road traced by them. So, to start, we propose a feasibility study, and the construction of a virtual model, of a Lagrange O'Neill City.

This project, like the previous two, can be proposed to universities for graduation works.

Choosing the best ones, we will pass to the second stage of the project, the construction of a virtual model, which will be virtually visited by everybody, and also bring some cash to support the Space Renaissance.

Different models should be traded-off: the O'Neill Cylinder concept, the Thorus concept proposed by Von Braun, and possible other models. The great vantage of any spinning structure, vs. Moon settlements, is the possibility to simulate the Earth gravity at periphery, while allowing zero G at the center of the structure.

At a more advanced stage of the project, shares of the future Lagrange City could be sold to share holders.

A major problem for orbital space settlements will be solar and cosmic radiation. Those problems should be specifically addressed by the designers.

The orbital space settlement could prove to be a major draw-card for popular interest in space, by potentially allowing investment in a concept that could be build. This may be in a form of share purchase, which would generate funding for research, development and construction. The essential design is very simple and a brochure could be made to invite investment when the virtual world model can be experienced. A sales office could be established in the virtual world, as well as in real life.

Many people have purchased block of land on the Moon, making millions of dollars for the people who ran or still run the schemes. Are these blocks real and realisable? How much more realistic an orbital space settlement proposal would be, which can be real and can be realised; and the market can extend as far as the interest grows, as any number of orbital space settlements can be built in space in the future. Shares purchased may be realised in the near future, or could become part of the family inheritance.

A major challenge for developing an orbital space settlement in a virtual world is the provision of a gravity that extends out in all directions from a central line. Once this gravity environment is available, if it is not already on the market (unable to find such a product yet), it will be possible to proceed with this project. Virtual world environments can be purchased off the shelf and the owners and users then proceed to develop the in-world environment to their own liking and wishes. In the same way, the provision of an orbital space settlement gravity environment could be an off-the-shelf product, which owners and users could then develop to their own likings and wishes. The product could be a virtual world of its own, as if in space, in which any number of orbital space settlements could be located, or, if possible, inserted into an existing virtual world as a sky box, which users can teleport into from the surface.

# Chapter II

The discussion

Day 1 – June 25th 2011
- Adriano Autino: today agenda:
 15.00 GMT
  a) chairperson election (Gail)
  b) approval of agenda (only members)
 15.30 GMT
  c) presentation of ISSUE I (AA)
  http://www.spacerenaissance.org/SRIC/ISSUE_I_ppt_PRESENTATION.pdf
 16.15 GMT
  d) open discussion on ISSUE I (all can post, asking the floor to the chairperson)
 17.00 GMT
  e) presentation of possible amendments to ISSUE I (members only)
 18.00 GMT
  f) adjourn

[17.00.25] Congress begin here – election of the chairperson
Gail B. Leatherwood is unanimously elected as chairperson.

[17.15.22] Presentation of Issue I – by A. V. Autino
I have to say something, firstly
I will not speak as an European, but as a Human Earthling
in my presentation i will move some hard criticism, mainly to the space policy of the last 40 years
such criticism is not addressed to any national responsibilities, it is to be intended as a global criticism to the Earth Space Spolicy, thugh of

course that was leaded but some main governments, who had the economic power to do it

so please take my words as a positive criticism, with the aim to reach a finally good and effective strategy, and work all together for the shared goals

now, please, if you didn't yet done, please download this file:

http://www.spacerenaissance.org/SRIC/SRIC_ISSUE_I_the_SRI_program_2011_2015.pdf

ok, the title says assuring survival, employment and a future for all of our childrens by bootstrapping the Solar Civiliaztion

Solar Civilization means a civilization targeted to expand into the Solar System

so this is our long term committment, water and life components are everywhere, inside the Oort cloud, where we live

Solar System is exactly at the center of a big snow ball, the Oort Cloud

there are trillions of comets all around us, we will never dye of famine nor thirst, in this corner of the Universe

as you all know, the Space Renaissance was created as pilosophical association, since our main task is to refound the human philosophy, completing the Copernican revolution

we are more environmentalist than environmentalists, since our concept of environment encompasses the whole solar system, and beyond

for example, we don't only care about our planet's surface environment, but also about the Earth's orbit, our interface to Cosmos

having said that, let's go to page two of the presentation, please

it is a small history of the Space Renaissance, from its very beginning in 2008

I think there's not much to add, when everybody will have read it

who are we? I am a small entrepreneur, in the field of computer science and systems engineering

the other founders... sorry, few more words about myself

I begun to think about the humanity future in 80s

i begun criticising the ecologist thought, that made a somehow shareable analysis but only proposed humanity to disappear, to save the planet

I made my first space advocacy web page in 1997, when i participated to the IAF congress in Torino

I met Patrick Collins in 1998, at the Melbourne IAF Congress, and Michael Martin Smith one year before

after that Patrick, Michael, Arthur, and many other friends kept on collaborating, until 2008, when Patrick and myself had this wonderful idea of the Space Renaissance

thinking about the 1500 Renaissance... we said, we would need some Medici families today...

and here we are

I think everybody know Patrick Collins, a true pioneer of Space Tourims and SBSP

during 2009 the SRI grew up, and many other friends joined us, Feng, for instance

We helped Feng to write an excellent paper, maybe the first serious temptative to make a criticism to the NASA policy

in that paper Feng pointed our how, after Apollo 11, NASA didn't have a strategic vision anymore

this position was recalled by the Jeff Greason speech at ISDC 2011

that paper is one of our milestones

however, let's go to page 3 please

the two main agencies, during 70's, didn't have a strategic focus on astronautics

ESA was mainly focused on telecommunication and Earth observing, and never joined the so-called 'astronautic club'

the astronautic club was made just by USA and URSS, for so many years

then China joined it, in 2003

the NASA strategy was focues on science and exploration, nobody talked about space industrialization

of course somebody did it: Kraffy Ehricke, and Gerard O'Neill, and Werber Von Braun... but all of their works remained closed in the drawers

Let's begin to say that , at SRI, our strategy is Astrnaoutics, i.e. Human Space Flight, that means:

- downsizing the cost to orbit (very preliminary urgent step)
- Space industrialization (settling firstly in the Geo-Lunar system, begin living and working overthere)
- conveing public support and private investments on the new space industry
- urging governments to develop the Space Based Solar Power
- developing a space policy harmonizing the interests of the people of the PostIndustrial Countries(POIC), of the New-Industrial Countries (NEIC), and of the Pre-Industrial (PRIC) ones

the above is in tune with what Jeff Greason stated: strategy has to be space settlement

without a strategy we will keep on going nowhere

our firts duty, as SRI, is to provide the best strategy, we can do it

we have the best philosophical elaboration of the whole space community

now, let's see where we are, and why we are here

page 4 please

oh, page 4 still spends some words about justification of our strategical points

a key world is 'industrialization'

that is a concret word, not just dreaming, not just eploration, not juset sending robots around...

downsizing the cost to orbit is the very first step, without that we will not go anywhere

conveying public support and private investments to the new space industry means go over the old diatribe between public and private: we need a choral effort

last but not least, we are an international association, we shall speak a language understandable by all the Earthling communities and people

we know perfectly that Americans and Europeans have different interests, respect Indians, Chinese, Brazilians

while we (post industrial countries) believe that we have solved the basic needs, and we care about environment, the new industrial people still have to get a car, a tv set, a refrigeratoir and a wash machine...

we are the Space Renaissance International

we have to talk to them as we talk to the post industrial people, and also to the pre-industrial ones

the Renaissance is for everybody, or it will never be

on page 5

a bit of history is necessary, to understand where we are, and why

in short: during 60's the focus was on Astronautics

we know why, the cold war imposed to demonstrate who was the best to win the space race

20% of the world was industrialized, and the space ocean (Earth's orbit) was clean

on page 6

from 70's to 2000, the focus changed, the big lobbies decided it was better to earn some money from space, and begun orbiting telecommunication satellites

the ISS was built, costing a lot, being on a wrong orbit, useless for any intermediate station, and repeating substantially what was already done n MIR

X15 was abandoned, and the space shuttle was built, in 5 unic pieces, without running an industrial development line, and avoiding to make a true RLV

the Scientific payloads took place as well

the focus was: Earth & Business

result: our space ocean was filled up of garbage

in the same time Earth's population reached 6 billions

page 7 is a realistic view of the 5500 tons of space debris currently orbiting around Earth

during the last ten years such an insane politics kept developing

nowadays we have large new economic powers on Earth

it means we are industrialized/ing maybe at 60-70%

you see the Earth is getting red, in the center of an iron cage

and the Earth's population is reaching 7 billions this year

we are in the middle of a process i'd call 'methaphysical warming' that's not exactly the 'golbal warming' refernced by many

it is made by many pereceptions, rights demand, environmental decay, resource wars, and fear of the future

page 8

to keep on supporting the development only on Earth would accelerate the implosion of the civilization, we do need with great urgency to boostrap the exo-development

page 9

to recover the space debris

btw, many of them could be used to build the orbiting infrastructure, to develop orbiting industry, hotel accomodations

to develop Moon infrastructures, and Lagrange Points ones

to start catching Near Earth Asteroids,

some of them are esier to reach than what people iamgine

the required delta V is very low

NEA are made of almost pure minerals, also precious metals

what do we need to do that?

here comes the hardest criticism

The lack of a strategy on astronautics, after the Moon landing, brought the civilization in the current situation: growing up and warming in an iron cage

on the long distance, we can say that Russians won the space race, since the old soviet Sojuz will be the only orbit vehicle, in the near future

China owns the US public debt, and is going to own more (Greece, for instance)

America had (and has) the best space technology, but lacking of a political strategical vision

Russia and China had a very bad politics.

Seems that having any political strategical vision is however better than having none vision

Simply thrust in technology, and its capability to affirm on the free market, doesn't work (of course it doesn't exist such a thing like a true free market, but only monopoles, lobbies and greedy commercial barriers...)

Even a bad politics won vs. a good technology.

Let's think about what a good politics could do.

!!!

now, let's go quickly to the end of this presentation...

following page (10, I think)

I just would like to recall these statements, that try to put in a good sort some of the development lines:

develop SBSP firstly to feed space customers

develop massive SBSP following Civilian Astronautics, not before, and not <u>instead of</u> Civilian Astronautics

we are all supporters of SBSP, but, should SBSP become the new 'telecommunication' business, we would have failed

we cannot bear other 40 years like the past ones

we need to fly, not just to fly robots

have you ever dream about flying, over valleys and seas?

It could mean it is written in our dna, maybe our ancestors used to fly, in zero g... we just want to go back home, maybe

on the following pages I recall the summary of the analysis contained in the book "Three Theses for the Space Renaissance"

That is the substance of the criticism to the XX Century ideologies, still dominant: both have clamorously failed

Chernobyl was the failure of the real socialist ideology

Gulf of Mexico and Fukushima are the failure of the liberist ideology

full stop, carriage return

we keep on voting for utopias, but we have in change the real liberism, with all of its greediness, monopoles, commercial barriers, and real socialism, with its lack of liberty, suppression of initiatives and of any excellence in the name of a supposed "collective good"

humanity is enough of such old ideologies

humanity needs renaissance

Space Renaissance

- Sergio Lebid: (clap)

- Julio Gonzalez: (clap)

- Rob Hunt: (clap)

- Dr. Feng Hsu: (clap)
- Krahazik Dragon: (clap)
- Anton Volkonskiy: (y)
- Kim Peart: Mighty Clap!!!
- Bahadır Hilmi ALPER: (clap)
- Adriano Autino: thank you very much,friends, you warm my heart
- Neda Ansari: Standing ovation.
- Dr. Feng Hsu: space renaissance is a new ideaology which must replace socialism and capitalism all together....SRI is not just about space, it's about sustainable human development and survival....
- Sergio Lebid: Excellent Adriano!!!
- G B Leatherwood: You've given us a lot of new and wonderful stuff to think about, Adriano. Now how do we make it happen?
- Scott Brown: Well done
- Arthur Woods: (y)
- Kim Peart: Strategically Gail, win the hearts and minds of 10 million people in ten years
- Adriano Autino: it is our duty, in this congress, to decide the very first steps we shall move
- Adriano Autino: starting from where we, the SRI, are now
- G B Leatherwood: OK, folks, we're running behind and I don't think Adriano has finished proposing what we do about what he's just said. Adriano?
- Adriano Autino: yes, i was just waiting for some comments incoming
- popov.alain: how about translating sbsp in as many languages as possible in wikipedia ?
- Neda Ansari: Translation of SBSP - excellent idea.
- popov.alain: just look how poorly it is done on all the earth languages
- Kim Peart: Connect SBSP with any move to deal with Earth problems - Geoengineering to deal with climate change, for instance
- Adriano Autino: - popov.alain:

<<< how about translating sbsp in as many languages as possible in wikipedia ?maybe making the Space Renaissance International voice on wikipedia would be a good thing too

- popov.alain: spanish lead on this one
- popov.alain: of course linking the concept to as many ideas as pissible
- popov.alain: possible sorry
- Sergio Lebid: At this point in history the masses are programmed by viral propaganda vis-avis, for example, YouTube, which gave birth to the likes of "justin bieber', etc...Our message to the masses globally must go viral
- popov.alain: and with pictures
- Adriano Autino: ok, let me turn the last two slides, then we will open the discussion
- SpaceShaft: Adriano it all sounded very inspirational, but I have some reservations regarding how to gather the fundings by the methods you suggest, for sure they are incompatible by the current objectives of the majority in the US congress (GOP). And regarding the EU, from my perspective they pretty much follow the US guidelines with historical delay od some years. Without going too far look at the complaints expressed by Secretary Gates regarding the EU investment in defence. If investing in defence is so affected by indiference what about other common goals? I do simpatize with seeking the political and financial support of individuals, political minorities and organizations (eg: greenpeace, development org., etc.). But the real thing is to find fundings for the SR Int. right otherwise ... ?
- Sergio Lebid: Yes Adriano, SRI on wikipedia and every conceivable viral news proliferation...
- G B Leatherwood: If I had a big gavel I'd be banging it so Adriano could finish his presentation. BANG! Adriano has the floor, please hold further comments until he finishes.
- Adriano Autino: thank you mr. chairman
- Adriano Autino: ok, our strategical address, for the next four year, until 2015, should be:
    - Boost the most promising space industrial development lines
    - Space Tourism, SubOrbital Tourism, Greater Earth region industrialization, Space Based Solar Power
    - protecting life in space from hard radiations, and artificial gravity

- Conveying financial support to the new space industry
- stimulate the growth of a new mass space industry
- international space investment funds
- tax discounts and friendly financing
- grants and incentives to hiring young graduated personnel and experienced personnel
- support to create new kind of companies, combining cultural, philosophical and
- artistic concepts toward astronautical services and jobs, including virtual space habitats, where people can imagine a life outside the gravitational well

- Adriano Autino:

what will we do?

Raising the public awareness of the urgency to downsize the cost to orbit

social-economic projects, large surveys, conferences, public events, outreach on media, new SRI website, blog

our strategy for the next four years (to be better discussed tomorrow):

Three Projects – exposed in Issue II
- Civilization Risk Assessment and Mitigation
- Detect the most promising space industrial development line
- Feasibility study and design of a virtual O'Neill habitat, to be settled at an earthMoon Lagrange Libration Point

when the projects will be described enough (WBS, WPD, estimation of costs), we will contact universities (a list of universities to be contacted shall be written) and then, having the endorsmenet of some universities, Seeking grants and sponsors, to seek grants from foundations, to seek sponsors and donors, to contact celebrities

in the same time, we have to Build the Space Renaissance International:

- a large membership campaign
- build the local chapters (North-America, Europe, Asia)
- creating the marketing network of the SRI affiliated entities

- Anton Volkonskiy: what about propusion science. Until we have new kinds of propusion - we will have expensive flights

- Adriano Autino: and, as Sergio said, a true viral campaign

- Adriano Autino:

A large outreach program
- organize conferences, with the SRI president and other choosen speakers
- make a new web site, and a blog
- write on media
- speak at other conferences (such as ISDC, NSS, etc...)

- Adriano Autino:

ok, that's all by me for today :)

we provided an analysis

we provided guidelines for a new space policy

we provided a plan for the SRI

- Sergio Lebid: (clap)

- Adriano Autino: it will be in our capabilities and initiative to realize it

- Kim Peart: Thanks Adriano

- Dr. Feng Hsu: Is it time now for comments?

- Adriano Autino: thanks also to the other friends who worked with me to the theses

- Kim Peart: Space Shaft (name?) - Political decisions and corporate direction are directly influenced by people in numbers

- Kim Peart: Have enough people demanding action on anything and action will follow

- Adriano Autino: yes, Gail, I think we can open the discussion

- Adriano Autino: it would be better to ask the floor to the chairman

[18.54.30] Open discussion on ISSUE I

- G B Leatherwood: Yes, Feng, the floor is now open for discussion. We'll take comments in the order they've been posted.

- Dr. Feng Hsu: The key is a PR strategy Adriano!! We must connect the SRI movement with the issues confronting the everyday lives of the general public...such as the energy shortages, climate changes, water & food shortages and Wars....or we will be seeing as irelevant organization for the small group of space fines....

- Neda Ansari: Agree with Dr. Hsu.

- Kim Peart: Start with basis survival issues - and identify what must happen

- Adriano Autino: @Feng, as we will discuss tomorrow, I think project 1 (Civilization Risk Assessment) includes all of the issues you mention

- Walter C. Putnam: The key to getting it done is organizing on every local level. We must each begin now to publicize this views and get as many people involved as possible. That means all of us -- through Facebook, Twitter, LinkedIn and whatever other means are available.

- Dr. Feng Hsu: For example, we must say that the SRI is a viable way to save the western or world civilization in terms of getting out of the current economic dead loop....

- Rob Hunt: I'm not sure scaring humans into space will work. Probably need to appeal to profit/gain rather than demise of Earth

- Neda Ansari: Adriano addressed PR in the closing remarks, though - getting in touch with celebrities will go a very long way.

- Adriano Autino: @Walter, very well put. To multiply our efforts is key. So far very few of us were active. Very important will be if many of us will start talking in the name of SRI

- Dr. Feng Hsu: Yes, the scary tactics will not work, we must educate general public that space is an Ocean for resources and new economic horizons....

- Kim Peart: Wheatsheaf - Agree - the ultimate profit beyond a sustainable presence in space, from where we will not fall back to Earth

- Adriano Autino: (Kim and Wheatsheaf... the two of you are from Australia :))

- Rob Hunt: so.... what is Adriano's alternative to his criticised economic ideologies?

- Neda Ansari: The ISDC 2012 registration form, by the way, it is held in D.C. next year: https://www.nss.org/cgi-bin/register/tdregister?$Origin=ISDC12

- Adriano Autino: @Rob, the alternative is exo-development, opposite to Earth-closed-development (that's not development, in fact, but only regression)

- Rob Hunt: Adriano, that's all well and good, but an Earth-based business will have to profit

- Adriano Autino: @Rob: recover space debris, downsize cost to orbit, industrialize the geo-lunar space region, mining NEA, build a Lagrange artificial city

- Adriano Autino: @Rob: the progressive business line, from Earth to space, is space tourism, starting with sub-orbital, and heading to orbital

- Dr. Feng Hsu: That's why I do not quite agree with Adriano about the view that if we make SBSP another commercial success like the ComSat and the telecom industry, then we have "failed"... The problem is that FAR BEFORE we make SBSP the kind of commercial success, we must have achieved LOW COST access to space and the space transportation capability and space tourism are atually closely interconnected with SBSP, agreed??

- Rob Hunt: Adriano, I'm not sure that the 5500 tonnes space junk is much of an atractive proposition to develop

- Adriano Autino: @Feng, we would have failed if we had other 40 years filling the orbit with iron machines and NOT developing astronautics

- Kim Peart: Rob - if you'd like to chase up - kimpeart@iinet.net.au - lobby for Australia to use resource bonanza to invest in SBSP

- Adriano Autino: that would be anothe Earth-based business, nothing more

- Rob Hunt: Adriano, surely a *tiny* one

- Dr. Feng Hsu: The KEY here for a succeessful PR on SRI is the "Economic issue" and "Energy issue" and issues will impact the daily lives of everyone on earth!!

- Adriano Autino: we shall develop SBSP, but together with astronautics, not alone

- Sergio Lebid: @Adriano - I agree with you

- Rob Hunt: SBSP is not universally supported as a good idea (is it?)

- Walter C. Putnam: @Rob, we need to open new ways of looking at Earth and the Cosmos, with shared values of humanity, rather than remaining locked into philosophies from the 19th and 20th centuries -- and, obviously, many from much earlier in human history.

- Adriano Autino: so, my point is: let's promote SBSP, but never forget the priority is to go outside, i.e. astronautics

- Rob Hunt: @Walter - yes, but what are those ways, specifically if not economic??

- Dr. Feng Hsu: Of course, together with RLV and Space Transportationa and Space Tourism... let's not prirotize Space tourism, RLV or affordable access to space because they are all integal part of the SRI movement....

- Kim Peart: Rob - SBSP sold as the way to mine excess carbon from the air could pay

- Adriano Autino: @Rob, 5500 tons of material in orbit is a value... they are already outside the gravitational well, so they will not cost anymore 20K$ per kg ...

- Adriano Autino: @Rob, of course not all the 5500 tons can be used, only the medium big sizes...

- Rob Hunt: @Adriano, but what will we make with such a small mass of material?

- Dr. Feng Hsu: SBSP is a tool in our vast toolbox for help achieving a solar civilization, so it is critically important.....that's why it is a better strategy to not prioritze these things...If we must prioritize, let put RLV as top priority

- Anton Volkonskiy: we need different kind of propulsion

- Kim Peart: Feng - I see SBSP as the key stepping stone beyond Earth, leading to space industry and space settlement

- Adriano Autino: @Feng, agree

- Bahadır Hilmi ALPER: Sorry I am new to SPACE RENAISSANCE.Does SPACE RENAISSANCE have regional c oordinators like the organisation Space Generation Advisory Council(SGAC)

- Anton Volkonskiy: to collect the old satellites

- Adriano Autino: @Bahadir, not yet, everything is to be built up

- Anton Volkonskiy: antigravity?

- Adriano Autino: we have many supporters, but low organization, so far

- Sergio Lebid: Firstly, the SRI Race to Space PR Campaign must go viral...it must be an agressive campaign

- Rob Hunt: All - surly the reason that Armstrongs steps were so successful was because there was a *very* specific goal set in a *very* specific time frame. We must do the same.

- Kim Peart: Anton - A serious move to build SBSP at an international level would drive a galaxy of improved and new propulsion systems

- Adriano Autino: @Rob, yes. I believe after Gulf of Mexico and Fukushima a key word is 'safety'

- Adriano Autino: that's why i propose the Civilization Risk Assessment project

- Walter C. Putnam: @Rob, For starters, those in this forum must share many of the same values and goals for space inititatives. The primary task is to bring others into this sphere of thinking. As you can see, as soon as we agree on something -- the goal -- we immediately get bogged down in debate over the details. So, we have to keep getting back to the common goal.

- Rob Hunt: SRI needs to be seen by the general human public as having a very tightly defined goal and timeframe, else it will be seen as fringe

- Kim Peart: Anton - I would appreciate any evidence that "antigravity" as a propusion system is possible

- G B Leatherwood: I have to stick something in here. On P. 3, under "Summarizing the SRI (near term) strategy" the first priority is "downsizing the cost to orbit." Without that, no SBSP or anything else.

- Sergio Lebid: @Walter - exactly!

- Sergio Lebid: @Gail - exactly!

- Dr. Feng Hsu: I fully agree with Kim: Anton - A serious move to build SBSP at an international level would drive a galaxy of improved and new propulsion systems

- Bahadır Hilmi ALPER: As it mentioned before translation into other languages is a good idea.I can make the Turkish translation of the documents on SBSP.

- Rob Hunt: All - so are we all agreeing that drastic reduction in cost to orbit is our clear goal?

- Krahazik Dragon: yes

- Kim Peart: Roib - we could work on that by setting an example in Australia

- Sergio Lebid: yes

- Adriano Autino: @Feng, and Kim, be careful with that confidence, the telecommunication business was run with spendable rockects, and made everyone happy for years...

- Bahadır Hilmi ALPER: And also the translation of thedocuments on SRI

- Adriano Autino: - Bahadır Hilmi ALPER:

<<< And also the translation of thedocuments on SRI

Great!

- Walter C. Putnam: Yes, Rob. It's sort of like the U.S. healthcare debate. Regardless of how we pay for it, unless the costs come down it will break us.

- Rob Hunt: All - can we break down the "lowering cost to orbit" goal into smaller achievable sub-goals?

- Dr. Feng Hsu: I would like to share a paper by my India friend about making SBSP a G20 issue....SBSP is perhaps the only economic issue will catch the G20 attention, I wish Space Tourism would as well but the G20 would not give a dime - too hard for them to understand the reasons behind, but ENERGY will do it !!!!

- Neda Ansari: I'll translate SBSP to Persian.

- Anton Volkonskiy: I have conducted some experiments on antigravity, but didn't have enough equipment - nobody beleives it, but my device lost 200% weight of its active zone. It didnt fly, but it seemed to be very possible...

- Dr. Feng Hsu: Great Neda, you are my hero!!

- Bahadır Hilmi ALPER: Maybe we can form a translation team together that would be more organisational

- Neda Ansari: This message has been removed.

- Bahadır Hilmi ALPER: :)

- Adriano Autino: - Bahadır Hilmi ALPER:

41

<<< Maybe we can form a translation team together that would be more organisational

Excellent idea, google groups are good for that

- Sergio Lebid: @Anton - Excellent! My group and I are also going to reveal some of our discoveries by year's end...

- Stephanie Lynne Thorburn: Yes we need to reduce costs to orbit-space tourism will otherwise be a preserve of the elite. As a whole, more investment is needed at all levels in the space industry and a greater public awareness of the utility of space to our common future (i.e.) sustainable energy solutions that are based on space based solar power..

- Sergio Lebid: @Stephanie - Exactly!

- Dr. Feng Hsu: @Adriano, your worry about SBSP becoming aother Telecom industry is not necesasry because, IT IS IMPOSSIBLE to achieving SBSP comemrcilization with any ELV or EELVs, IT MUST BE RLVs ....I am a member if the Solar-high group www.solarhigh.org and we have been studying this economic and technical issues for the entire past year.....

- Anton Volkonskiy: I need to conduct some experiments in ZeroG

- Adriano Autino: @Feng, i am very much inetersted to know more about that, could you indicate some papers to me?

- Adriano Autino: (it would be a bless of God if SBSP needs astronautics to be realized...)

- Dr. Feng Hsu: Yes, I will.....

- Kim Peart: Thanks Anton

- Adriano Autino: Friends, let me recall something that i take of great importance, seeing the SRI experience so far

- Bahadır Hilmi ALPER: @Adriano Autin,nedaansari Forming a group for translation is a nice idea it will be a good start

- Adriano Autino: we should agree all together that we shall take initiative as SRI

- Anton Volkonskiy: Lets vote

- Adriano Autino: each one of us can of course pursue their own projects, and sue the SRI to enhance them

- Kim Peart: Anton - pleased to be kept abreast - another reason for space development

- Adriano Autino: but very important is that each one of us start taking intiative as a SRI member

- Dr. Feng Hsu: If we talk about economic impact to human development on earth or in space, SBSP should be a top issue on the SRI aganda....simply because RLV and space transpoartation is the No.1 obstacle humans must overcome for any commercial applications....

- Stephanie Lynne Thorburn: As as whole, I would like to take the opportunity of congratulating Adriano and the many industrious members of the SRI at all levels on what has actually been achieved in a relatively short space of time within the Space Renaissance. The organisation actually encompasses affiliations and support from a wide sector of the space industry. Progress at all levels is always difficult in times of recession and investment and improvements are always possible in an organisationals sense; but the SRI always shows initiative - initiatives such as this Congress are very innovative.

- Adriano Autino: signing their articles as members of the Space Renaissance International

- Anton Volkonskiy: yes

- Walter C. Putnam: Yes. Agreed.

- Adriano Autino: when some of us speaks at a conference, say that is a member of the SRI

- Adriano Autino: and put a link to the SRI website on the home pages of all our websites

- Krahazik Dragon: My efforts are in developing a working PDRE system for use on launch systems.

- Kim Peart: Stephanie - An international commitment to build the infrastructure of space - the SBSP stations - will deliver flight systems and tourism will be a lucritive spin-off industry

- Sergio Lebid: @Stephanie - I concur with you that Adriano and others have done an enormous degree of progress with little resources!

- G B Leatherwood: @krahazik: What is "PDRE?"

- Krahazik Dragon: Pulse Detonation Rocket Engine

- Adriano Autino: Gail, someone proposed to vote

we should see if somebody wants to propose amendments

however we will vote the final text only in two weeks, integrating possible amendments even during such time interval

- Sergio Lebid: @Adriano - I agree

- Rob Hunt: I have to sign off and sleep - TNX Adriano, Gail and everyone - great things happening here. See you tomorrow. Rob ;)

- Sergio Lebid: Good night Rob Hunt

- Adriano Autino: Bye Rob, thanks for your contribute

- Dr. Feng Hsu: Dr. Kalam of former India president is a strong proponent for an International Committee on SBSP inittiatives.... I may be visiting India in the next month or so, should I speak for the SRI that we support such inititative with strongest conviction possible?

- G B Leatherwood: Adriano, thanks. I wasn't sure if that was a motion, and if so, what it was we were to vote on. Anton?

- Adriano Autino: @Feng, wholeheartedly yes

- Kim Peart: Bye Rob - hope we can catch up!!!

- Dr. Feng Hsu: great Adriano

- Anton Volkonskiy: that we all agree with philosophical understanding of the status of civilization and the SRI political program 2011 – 2015

- Rob Hunt: @Kim email me: rghunt@tpg.com.au

- Neda Ansari: That is fantastic Feng!

- Sergio Lebid: @Feng - That is great!

- Keith Henson: I wish someone would do an analysis of space tourism. I have tried hard to make it work and failed

- Keith Henson: the numbers just didn't work, not even when all the transport development was paid for by an sbsp project

- G B Leatherwood: One moment. It has been moved by Anton Volkonsky that we agree with the philosophical understanding of the status of civilization and the SRI political program 2011-2015. Is there a second to the motion?

- Sergio Lebid: I second

- Walter C. Putnam: Is it OK to share this SRI document you briefed us on today. I'd like to go ahead and post a link.

- Keith Henson: sure

- Kim Peart: Feng - I was reading that the NSS was working with folk in India to develop SBSP

- G B Leatherwood: It has been moved and seconded as stated. Is there further discussion?

- Adriano Autino: the whole paper is on the sri website, i'll give you the link...

- *** Dr. Feng Hsu sent Non_Profit_IPPP_Foundation_for_an_International_SSP_Mission-.doc ***

- Keith Henson: unfortunately I don't think it is strongly connected to the real world of available technology and economics

- *** Dr. Feng Hsu sent Strategic_Development_SSP_with_Feng_06-15-2011-.doc ***

- Adriano Autino: sorry, let's pay attention to the chairman

- Adriano Autino: then we can exchange files

- Dr. Feng Hsu: Yes, Kim but very little progress has been made so far. NSS is a US centric organization so it's vison are somewhat limited.....

- Stephanie Lynne Thorburn: 'The status of civilisation' I read and agree with a majority of; but the philosophical observations are subjective essentially. The SRI political programme is more policy based and contains some evocative goals to work towards, both organisationally for the SRI and in terms of space advocacy.

- G B Leatherwood: There is a motion on the floor. Any discussion must relate to that motion before any other discussion will be recognized.

[19.39.21] Voting on Issue I

- Adriano Autino: please, could you restate the motion?

- Anton Volkonskiy: we agree with the philosophical understanding of the status of civilization and the SRI political program

- G B Leatherwood: The motion is: It has been moved by Anton Volkonsky that we agree with the philosophical understanding of the status of civilization and the SRI political program 2011-2015.

- Keith Henson: Feng, that's not the biggest problem with NSS

45

- G B Leatherwood: Keith, you're out of order. Please hold that discussion until after the vote.

- Keith Henson: do you want us to indicate agreement?

- Walter C. Putnam: second the motion

- Adriano Autino: say AYE or NAY

- Stephanie Lynne Thorburn: What are the key areas being outlined in the document for agreement?

- Kim Peart: Agreed Gail - ammendments can happen as new information arrives

- Walter C. Putnam: Aye

- Julio Gonzalez: aye

- Anton Volkonskiy: aye

- Kim Peart: YES

- Sergio Lebid: AYE

- Nebojsa Stanojevic: aye

- Adriano Autino: @Stephanie: the ones recalled in my today's presentation

- Sean Con: aye

- Keith Henson: ave, though I think it is not particularly influential

- Keith Henson: any nays?

- Neda Ansari: aye

- Adriano Autino: i don't vote since it was my paper

- Jennifer Bolton: aye

- G B Leatherwood: Seems that we've already voted, so are there any "nays?"

- G B Leatherwood: Hearing none, the "ayes" have it. Voting is closed.

- Kim Peart: Great!

- G B Leatherwood: We are nearing the end of our time, so is there any further discussion? Adriano? What about tomorrow?

- Walter C. Putnam: Good work, Mr. Chairman. Visionary leadership, Adriano.

- Adriano Autino: I promised the link of the Issue I to Walter, here it is:

http://www.spacerenaissance.org/SRIC/SRIC_ISSUE_I_the_SRI_program_2011_2015.pdf

- Kim Peart: Keith - Space tourism will skyrocket - especially for long stay - with the constuction of an Earth-gravity orbotal space settlement

[19.47.41] ADJOURNING

Day 2 – June 26th 2011

[17.00.26] Congress begin here – election of the chairperson

Gail B. Leatherwood was elected as chairperson

[17.13.54] Agenda of Day 2

- G B Leatherwood: The agenda for today is the same as yesterday except that Adriano will be presenting "Issue II," which is the three projects approach to making our work successful. Adriano, you have the floor any time you're ready.

[17.15.17] PRESENTATION OF ISSUE II – BY A. V. AUTINO

- Adriano Autino: could you please download this document:

http://www.spacerenaissance.org/SRIC/SRIC_ISSUE_II_Three_Projects.pdf

- Adriano Autino: ok,Mr. Chairman, I'd begin my presentation, may I have the floor?

- G B Leatherwood: You have the floor.

- Adriano Autino:

http://www.spacerenaissance.org/SRIC/SRIC_ISSUE_II_Three_Projects.pdf

well, yesterday we focused our analysis of the status of civilization, and our strategy to keep the civlization in development, avoiding a possible implosion

we stated that our strategy is astronautics, priority to downsize the cost to orbit, soliciting both government help and private investments having well present that human spaceflight and geo- lunar space industrialization shall come in the highest priority

within space industrialization we support SBSP, as a solution to provide energy both to space customers and to Earth

always having present that SBSP shall be developed together with astronautics, and not alone, or instead astronautics, otherwise it could repeat the process of telecommunication during past 40 years

at this point, Feng made an important comment: that it would not be possible, since SBSP needs RLV technologies, and needs astronautics, for its development

I would kindly suggest Feng maybe he might prepare an amendment on this subject, that I take of great relevance for our strategy and position

having said the above, let's go to the today discussion

while we have a well defined political proposal, if we want to develop and incisive campaign, we need something concret

allowing us to get in touch with interlocutors in the academic world, with foundations, with communities engaged in social projects, inside and outside the space community

i'd say mostly outside, since our duty is to reach the real planet Earth communities, not just the communities that are ready to listen and understand us

therefore we thought about one project

then, discussing with Alberto, we came to think two projects were better...

and, seeing the great idea proposed by Kim, we definitely understood that three was a perfect number :)

I will just recall the titles, then i will propose a possible roadmap

1) Civilization Risk Assesment & Management Project

2) Detect the most promising space industrial development line

3) Feasibility study and design of a virtual O'Neill habitat, to be settled at an earth- Moon Lagrange Libration Point

as you can see, we are not talking about technological projects, the third one is the most 'technological' of the three we aim to involve not only the university faculties of engineering and science, but also economics, sociology, philosophy, humanistic faculties

we want to put not only technicians, but also philosophers at work, on this projects

this will be, in itself, a wall-breaking thing

those people don't expect to be called to work on space issues

but we will put them in face of their responsibility, with project 1: the civilization is at risk, what is your risk mitigation plan?

the second project is more suitable to be proposed to economics faculties

it is a tradeoff, targeted to detect the best promising space business development line

analyising several lines, such as space suborbital and orbital tourism, asteroids mining, moon industrialization, orbital industries, Lagrange platforms, try to support by figures (not just impressions or scientific knowlegdes) which idnustrial development line will allow market and industry to grow up togetehr

supporting each other in a progressive way

the thirs project is fascinating, maybe Kim will like to add something about that

we will propose to design and develop a virtual O'Neill City to be placed at Lagrange L1

people will have the possibility to visit it in a virtual reality frame

many commercial sub projects could derivate from that, games, for instance

that could become a relevant source of financial funding

so, this is the general picture of the three projects

how will we proceed?

step 1 will be to prepare applications for all the foundations who give grants for social projects

we will try to get some money, in order to pay at least some expenses, when we will have to travel to meet universities, and possible partners

step 1, also will include the preparation of the Statements of Work, a draft WBS, a work packages description, an idea of the costs

costs will also depend on how many universities will accept our proposal, and how they will decide to develop it

we should also be prepared to many projects to be developed for each type...

maybe some universities will accept to collaborate with other ones, maybe not, that's not important

the importrant is that these projects will be developed, in partenrship with the SRI

we will be called to hold conferences, likely

this will be part of the viral comapign suggested by Sergio, yesterday

step 1 includes also the rpeparation of a plan, with a list of the foudnations and of teh universities to involve

step 2 we will move toward universities, and collect their availability to develop the projects

we will propose to the universities to give our themes as graduation works to some of their students or to create work teams, to develop the projects

step 2 will also include the preparation of a questionnaire, to be developed in project 1, a social questionnaire, about the risks of the civilization, and what will be the posisble mitigation actions

step 3 is the development of the projects

during step 3 we whould be launched enough to reach celebrities and important donors

that will be the moment we will seed our idea of the Medici Space Foundation, and maybe begin to create the seed funds for that

a first milestone will be 2013, two years from now

in june 2013 we should have the three projects well routed, maybe some of thema already arrived to some conclusions

having some data about the real probability of the risks, we will be able to run other large surveys, this time based on a scientific work, nomore just on the words of Stephen Hawking, though fully respectable of course

maybe, before analysing in detail each one of the three projects, we might open the discussion on the general setup?

[18.05.03] Open discussion on ISSUE II

- G B Leatherwood: First, what are your questions about what has been presented so far?

- Adriano Autino: my questions:
    a. do we think that a strategy based on foundations / universities / surveys will be the best, to develop the Space Renaissance?
    b. do we think that these three ideas of projects are good enough for the above goal?
    c. is the proposed roadmap good enough?

- Rob Hunt: general setup sounds good, but the three projects vary markedly in their palatability to the public/universities/interests. Project III seems easiest and most attractive for economic interests and development, I see Project II being quite achievable, but Project I will get bogged down in argument

- Adriano Autino: - Rob Hunt:

   <<< will get bogged down in argument - please say it in plainer words for a non English mother tongue...

- Sergio Lebid: I commend you Adriano and Contributors to this as this has a very firm base to launch SRI to a much higher level of attention and activities...yes, the proposed roadmap is excellent

- Keith Henson: bogged down, run into too many problems

- Bruce Mackenzie: Proposal 3, the Virtual Space Settlement, has some similarities with some Space efforts in Second Life (SL), but is much more extensive. We should check what has already been done in SL, for example, by Cheryl and Bryce of NSS- Oregon. Note we could use OpenSim, which is free if someone has access to a internet server.

- Rob Hunt: sorry - Project I will become argued by politicians / historians / scientists and no clear answer come out

- Rob Hunt: @brucemacknz - agreed

- Adriano Autino: well, I am aware that it is extremely difficult to get a really objective picture, with project 1, but however we will put our feet in the dish, posing the problem of the global risk, and its space solution

- Walter C. Putnam: Isn't the main thrust of project one to get people involved, though, rather than to reach a conclusion?

- *** Adriano Autino added Fred Becker ***

- Stephanie Lynne Thorburn: I think the civilisation risk assessment concept is to really enable the public to see space development as a viable option to circumvent our vulnerability considering recent social/environmental events. Will the SRI remain a non- profit organisation throughout the development of these three quite ambitious projects?

- Adriano Autino: each project will have more than one goal, a primary one and secundary ones

- Kim Peart: I wonder if a Think Tank could be the way to pursue the projects and gain institutional and political support - as well as industry

- Adriano Autino: we will aim to the main, but will be happy if some of the secundary ones will be reached

- Sergio Lebid: @Keith, Potential problems have solutions with a concrete level of common interest and cooperation

- Sergio Lebid: I agree with you Adriano, always aim high!

- Adriano Autino: @Stephanie, yes the SRI will remain a non profit
 we will see if will be convenient/useful to create other comemrcial entities when needed

- Bruce Mackenzie: as for getting universities involved, especially for students to work on space projects as graduation requirements - these are called: Thesis, or CapStone, or 'qualifying projects' - at the Mars Foundation, I have been trying to get this to happen for a while, and have learned it is best to get a faculty member involved first, some funding helps, ... if you get students interested first, they may be unable to find a faculty member willing to be the academic advisor. When I approached a university office or department first, they wanted major funding from the beginning, which is not worth it. ... conclusion - interest the professors first.

- Adriano Autino: @Bruce, agree, I was thinking the same

- Sergio Lebid: @Bruce, that has been my expereince also with my projects when approaching universities...

- Dr. Feng Hsu: I think Kim's idea of forming a SRI think tank is excellent suggestion,....SRI can remain non profit but SRI think tank could be for-profit.... either way, we must resolve the funding issue....

- SpaceShaft: I completelly agree with Bruce, I keep trying at local universities, and all I do is spend $$$

- Sergio Lebid: Funding, funding, funding will be the driving force, especially during these times

- G B Leatherwood: @Bruce: Good point. As a Jet Propulsion Laboratory "Solar System Ambassador" I ran headon into this problem, and the same thing trying to start a high school chapter of NSS. The problem is not the kids, of any age, but the rigid curricula and finding a faculty member to sponsor outside or even classtime activities.

- Kim Peart: A Not For Profit organisation can receive large funding

- Jesús Raygoza: I do also think Kim's idea of forming a SRI think-tank is a good one.

- G B Leatherwood: However, we have a faculty member at Azabu University in Japan, Dr. Patrick Collins, Professor of Environmental Economics. Surely he can help us.

- Fred Becker: If funding is a focus, we can look at what space groups have been most successful getting funding or projects going. X- Prize is one of those.

- Sergio Lebid: @Gail, exactly!... Professors have access to grant opportunities

- Stephanie Lynne Thorburn: @Bruce, I agree that involving senior people is best first, as university faculties in my experience are reluctant and do not always get involved if idea originate outside their own departments.

- Adriano Autino: we already have a non profit organization: the Space Renaissance International, having an Italian VAT number and everything what needed

- Sergio Lebid: @Fred, exactly!

- Adriano Autino: @Kim, what should be a Think- Thank?

- Bruce Mackenzie: I suggest the SRI should NOT work on #1, because a) risks are well known, b) SRI can get side- tracked, and spend too much time documenting Earth- based risks, c) emphasizing negative aspects is not a good modivator for people, ... instead we should (1) just list the risks, and (2) spend all our efforts on off- planet SOLUTIONS to the risks.

- Sergio Lebid: With the appropriate viral PR campaign, fundraising will thrive

- Rob Hunt: @brucemack - yes!

- Walter C. Putnam: @Adriano, SRI is already a Think Tank and a non- profit. What is needed is the funding.

- Jesús Raygoza: Yes, Gail, the regular problem is the rigid (but, many times incompetent) rigid curricula and finding a faculty memeber to spondor outside or even classtime activieties. Same problem in Mexico.

- Kim Peart: Investigation of Think Tanks - there are diverse examples

- Sergio Lebid: @Jesus, exactly and this is a global problem!

- G B Leatherwood: Bruce: I, too, am afraid this might become a climate change kind of thing with armed camps on both sides of any issue. could waste a lot of time and energy. Like the idea of proposing solutions to the known problems.

- Fred Becker: So Peter Diamandis should be here. Is he on this conference today?

- Neda Ansari: @Waltputnam - exactly! Hi everyone :)

- Dr. Feng Hsu: Adriano, after listening your three projects, and I agree with your thoughts. However, before any of the three project get started, we must address two most pressing and practical projects: (1) our PR plan and projects to get more people to even know about SRI and its goals, (2) a drive for funding which will make things move... agreed???

- Sergio Lebid: @Feng, AGREED

- Rob Hunt: @Feng - agreed

- Adriano Autino: @Feng, agree. The two things should support eachother. The projects will make us be better known, and give us possibility to contact foundations to get grants

- Adriano Autino: I conceived the project as a tool to move ahead

- G B Leatherwood: Feng, et al., that's what Issue I was all about. Issue II projects will come after we get some of the Issue I items underway.

- Stephanie Lynne Thorburn: @Feng. Yes, sensible. These three projects are evocative, but the concrete PR and funding needs to be there first.

- Adriano Autino: we cannot somply go to donors and say: we are the SRI, give us some money

- Kim Peart: Gail - on the basis of the Precautionary Principle, it is possible to consider all possible risks and have plans drawn up to deal with each level of risk

- Sergio Lebid: @Adriano, your conceived tool is sound and now we must aggressively move forward!

- Adriano Autino: they will ask suddendly: what are you doing?

- Adriano Autino: and we will give them the SOW of our projects...

- Rob Hunt: SOW???

- Sergio Lebid: @Stephanie, Exactly!

- Adriano Autino: SOW = Statement of Work

- SpaceShaft: Have anyone thought about getting a bunch of eng among us and work on a practical application which could generate some cash by either demonstrating something that could be supported not only by the SRI but also by public money, DARPA, or any other org. Perhaps even trying to go into some Centenial Challenges?

- G B Leatherwood: Ah, sorry. Misspoke. Issues I and II can work together

- Sergio Lebid: @Gail, Yes

- SpaceShaft: to me all what I hear here is very idealistic but with little that could actually convince anyone but a writter of scifi

- Neda Ansari: @Spaceshaft - we are moving on a blog idea.

- Rob Hunt: does Project III have the best potential to get started quickly and possibly bring in some money?

- Adriano Autino: @Nelson, I respectfully disagree. The risk is real, and the space business development lines we are talking about are already in place (some) and could be in few years (others)

- SpaceShaft: I don't want to sound negative but I'm not really very philosophical and I feel I have heard these arguments before.

- SpaceShaft: INeda, I can see that

- Dr. Feng Hsu: Yesm issue I&II can certainly work together.... Issue I alone will not be enough for the PR and funding... that's why we need a PR PLAN and FUND RAISING PLAN to move forward....

- Sergio Lebid: @Feng, Exactly!

- Stephanie Lynne Thorburn: @friendly_nelson. It depends on how sci fi is presented- organisational PR that captures the imagination, so long as there is some stragegy involved too can be effective.

- Rob Hunt: @Feng - PR plan very important

- Walter C. Putnam: @Feng, We need a fund raiser. Does anyone have experience in this?

- Adriano Autino: @Feng, PR Plan and Fund Raising Plan... I would love if some of us came up with concret proposals (these are the kind of things my mind is not structured to think about...)

- Kim Peart: Nelson - the basic engineering work of telling the story that inspires the descion to act on serious space development is yet to happen

- Sergio Lebid: The basic essentials needed : (1) Viral PR Campaign (2) This will then trigger FUNDING

- Dr. Feng Hsu: a PR PLAN and FUND RAISING PLAN should be integrated activity or project

- Rob Hunt: @Sergio/Feng - good way to go

- Adriano Autino: However we have the basis to start: a rich web site (in progress of restyling), a non profit association

- G B Leatherwood: I think what is being said is that any PR plan has to have something concrete to present, otherwise it's just flash with no substance.

- Sergio Lebid: @Rob, feng and I are teleporting brilliant thoughts...:)

- Adriano Autino: @Gail, exactly. the projects try to fit this requirement

- Sergio Lebid: @Gail, sorry, but obviously

- Bruce Mackenzie: we are being too negative ... #3, the Virtual Space Settlement - is a good idea, even if we only did the minimum work to create a detailed 3D digital representation, we could create good graphics and animation flying through the settlement - the visual experience really helps to get new people's attention, and to get our message out to the interested public. summary - a .jpg (picture) is worth 1024 bytes of .txt (words)

- Rob Hunt: @Gail - also true, so we need to pick the ripest ideas that the public/universities will swallow, and integrate into PR?Funding attempts

- Jennifer Bolton: Project 3 - virtual space station model would be a useful promotional tool in PR campaign

- Rob Hunt: @brucemack - yeah baby!

- Sergio Lebid: @Bruce, Exactly!

- Stephanie Lynne Thorburn: Yes, virtual space station a v. good concept.

- Rob Hunt: @jennifer - agreed

- Sergio Lebid: @Jennifer, Exactly!

- Fred Becker: National Space Society is planning a PR campaign to promote space settlement. I will be sure we coordinate campaigns in some way.

- Sergio Lebid: @Fred, Super!

- Jesús Raygoza: I agree with Dr. Feng. No funds, no nothing! (y)

- Neda Ansari: Thanks Fred!!

- Rob Hunt: the PR campaign using Virtual Hab is the bait for funding/popularity

- Fred Becker: There is a virtual space settlement already created here. www.youtube.com/watch?v=oazFe2jbMxw.

- Kim Peart: Fredspace - collaborations in a wider movement will be essential to maximise success potential

- Dr. Feng Hsu: That's why we almost need a "Business Plan" for the SRI although it's a non- profit org, any group activities and goal- driven endeavors need a BUSINESS PLAN

- Bruce Mackenzie: @Fred Spacer, I am on some NSS committees, and am not sure which NSS PR campaign you mean, perhaps the Space Ambassador's , which will not amount to much because NSS expects the volunteers to create their own material to present to the public, with no coordination to share material, incidentally, I signed up for it, anyway.

- Sergio Lebid: @Kim, collaboration and cooperation always!

- Walter C. Putnam: I believe these three projects can proceed simultaneously. We can coordinate with others - - and create our own virtual space station.

- Sergio Lebid: @Walter, Agreed!

- Sergio Lebid: @Scott, Please elaborate...

- Scott Brown: It is not concret enough for me.

- Scott Brown: I believe we need something that is real not virtual i.e. Spaceport

- Kim Peart: Thanks for that Fred - lots of research needed - find out what the full state of play is - all hints welcome

- Sergio Lebid: @Scott, Yes, but real costs money

- Adriano Autino: I am seeing Habitat 2 on youtube... it's wonderful...

- Fred Becker: The NSS space settlement PR campaign is new Bruce. It is coming from the Public Affairs Committee (also new). It will kick off in the fall.

- Scott Brown: Real is how you get money. People of the world are ready for real programs, plan and real.

- Rob Hunt: @Scott - agreed, but we can capture the imagination of youth which will help the viral popularity we're after

- Krahazik Dragon: Virtual is a bit more dooable and less expensive in the short term and can be used as a steping stone leading up to real

- Sergio Lebid: @Scott, Agreed!

- Scott Brown: We have the imagination of the youth of the world what we do not have is a plan that captures more than their imagination

- Sergio Lebid: @krahazik, Exactly!

- Adriano Autino: @Dragon, you hit the point, exactly

- Rob Hunt: @Scott - you really think we have the imagination of the worlds youth??

- Adriano Autino: we discussed about embarking or not in technical projects

- Scott Brown: Yes, they are just tired of waiting for us to do something.

- Dr. Feng Hsu: We should approach some angel donners or investors who supports what we do and is willing to put up some financial support for us to start a PR campaign....We need $s or Euros to start a tangible PR campaign and we need professional advice....For instance, we must produce a short video to put up on our SRI site and on YouTube as well....

- Fred Becker: If we want to involve the youth, then let's activate them via the Space Generation Foundation. It is ready- made for this?

- Krahazik Dragon: A virtual office as a bas eof operations and meeting place with a loby people can visit an dlook around see whats going on, read the material, see the presentations with links to real world activities and results

- Bruce Mackenzie: as for #2 "2.2. Detect the most promising space industrial development " - this is very important, but how does SRI fit in ? many space entrepreneurs are working on promising space industries ... Can SRI help disseminate info ? provide publicicty? restart 'Space Business Roundtables' from the 1980's? Can we help identify Angel/VC funding and match to entrepreneurs? But, how can we do it any better than the existing groups, such as the 'Space Venture Forums" ?

- Adriano Autino: the SRI was not born to be a technical association

- Stephanie Lynne Thorburn: Involving young people is beneficial as the SRI are essentially involved with concepts to assist in our future and promoting science & technology developments.

- Rob Hunt: @Feng - great idea

- Sergio Lebid: @Feng, Exactly!

- Adriano Autino: it is a philosophical association

- Kim Peart: In finance - the futures market is about future predicted possibilities - which become more real when realised - but no absolute surety

- Walter C. Putnam: @Scott, I think we are all talking about the same thing. We need to tell people "We are going to build a space station - - and this is what it is going to look like."

- Adriano Autino: we take care of astronautics anthropology, retaking the work of Ehricke and O'Neill

- SpaceShaft: @Adriano: A philosophical association can fund practical projects, any ideas?

- Sergio Lebid: @Walter, Exactly!

- Sergio Lebid: @nelson, Exactly!

- Adriano Autino: we have to fill a lack of philosophical elaboration that brought the civilization where it is, in a cul de sac

- Rob Hunt: @Walter - yes

- Adriano Autino: @Nelson, sure, we can, after we will have funded our priority projects

- Stephanie Lynne Thorburn: @Feng. Yes, a short video and a short precis of what the SRI represent, core values/ aims would help in addition to well- constructed pdf documents.

- Adriano Autino: we need to talk to normal people of this planet

- Krahazik Dragon: SecondLife could be used as a virtual medium in conjunction with the website.

- Rob Hunt: @Adriano - I'm still worried about your continued reference to the world being doomed. Not sure that's a good thing to work around

- Sergio Lebid: All correct points however to get to the first base: (1) Agressive Viral PR campaign

- Anton Volkonskiy: Space station at GEO? with protective MF, Solar PS, will cost a fortune to deliver on chemical rockets

- Walter C. Putnam: @Sergio - Yes

- Adriano Autino: people needs to dream (the virtual space habitat is for this) people need to know about the future (projects one and two are for this requirement)

- G B Leatherwood: Please keep in mind that SRI isn't going to build the real space city- - we're going to support the establishment of a virtual space city where others can experiment that may lead to the real thing.

- Sergio Lebid: @Adriano, Yes

- Sergio Lebid: @Gail, Exactly!

- Adriano Autino: @Rob, people are not kids, the entertainers plaid them for a fool for long time

   now people is taking initiative, and want to be owner of their destiny

- Walter C. Putnam: @Gail, Yes. By "we" I mean the human race.

- SpaceShaft: @Adriano, I agree with that, and we that are capable of so doing, that is great. But most of the people need inspiration.

- Anton Volkonskiy: GEO station will be a step to a Moon station

- Rob Hunt: @Adriano, I agree with all you say, just don't think the developed world will take any notice of anyone who tells them the world is doomed unless they go into space

- Sergio Lebid: @nelson, SRI will provide inspiration...

- Adriano Autino: @Anton, we have to enter details of projects, yet

- Scott Brown: Space ship Earth is sinking and it seems we are arranging the deck furniture and carrying on academic virtual assignments that have been done and done by others. We need to do something that is unique, gutsy, and real.

- Rob Hunt: we should sell the positives of solving earthly issues, without the 'end of the world' flavour

- Adriano Autino: @Rob the so- called developed world is falling into a nightmare, faster than what we expected...

- Sergio Lebid: the Viral PR Campaign is critically required to provide positive inspiration...nothing negative!!!

- Adriano Autino: think about Ireland, Greece, Portugal, ...

- Rob Hunt: @Adriano - I'm not convinced of that, at all

- Krahazik Dragon: I agree Sergio

- Neda Ansari: I have to agree 100% with Rob.

- SpaceShaft: @sergio; but you will need something to show, young people like gadgets and not philosopy

- Dr. Feng Hsu: A short video should connect SRI's goal & activities with everyone's life, such as the space- based economy is perhaps the ONLY WAY to save the western economy and breaking the paradigm of the estern world producing and selling and the western world simply buying and comssuming which is a deadly economic trape for us all.... So, we will then understand SBSP, Space Tourism and next gen space transportation etc. will help us breaking the current economic dead-loop

- Krahazik Dragon: True SpaceShaft

- Walter C. Putnam: @Sergio - Agreed. There will always be negative aspects. We have to move forward.

- Rob Hunt: @Adriano - every generation/decade has had it's world-ending issues. the world is still here and an amazing place with amazing potential

- Kim Peart: Anton - the orbital space settlement will be the stepping stone to the whole Solar System and beyond
- Krahazik Dragon: even a plac ein Sl would need interactive content tog rab peoples interest, otherwise they would just glance around right quick then TP out
- Anton Volkonskiy: @Kim sure
- Sergio Lebid: @Nelson, I am a scientists first and one must be a philospoher to be a good scientist...gadgets are abundant in my portfolio and i agree with you but it starts with philospohy until we get FUNDING
- Anton Volkonskiy: @Kim but SS at GEO will provide SBSP station as well
- Adriano Autino: @Anton, we are talking about L1, not GEO
- SpaceShaft: @Sergio, that's ok for us but not for the public
- Anton Volkonskiy: ok
- Kim Peart: Exactly Sergio - Inspiration
- Sergio Lebid: @Nelson, the gadgets introduced to the masses begin as philosophical concepts...
- Neda Ansari: @Rob - that's awesome. Maybe we can collaborate on an SRI Children's book/CD project. That's what the children need!
- Jesús Raygoza: Yes, Adriano, the so- called developed countries are going to fall much faster in about a short period of time. As much as we push for Space development, perhaps we are going to convince many relevant people around the world for avoiding this fall (and underdeloped countries could fall into plain poverty).
- Fred Becker: We might consider the virtual space settlement as a "gadget" for demo purposes.
- Rob Hunt: as a general observation, we're all in furious agreement about many aspects of the 3 projects...
- Sergio Lebid: @Fred, Yes
- Walter C. Putnam: @Rob - We seem to agree on more than we disagree on
- Sergio Lebid: @Rob, Yes
- Kim Peart: Nadia - have a look at the interactive iPad books
- Sergio Lebid: @Jesus, yes

- Adriano Autino: @Jesus, yes, this our task. To do that we need projects, PR plan, etc... but I will never agree to contribute saying to the people 'everything will be allright...", this lullaby is taking people to sleep, and not to react to the global risk

- Rob Hunt: a round- table 'think tank' with pens and butvhers paper suggests itself to me

- Neda Ansari: Oh yes - - ipad...rings a bell :)

- Sergio Lebid: @Adriano, Yes, but with the emphasis on inspiring rather gloom and doom

- Rob Hunt: @Sergio - yes, yes, yes

- Walter C. Putnam: The main thing we seem to disagree on is whether anyone will support us with the framework Adriano has presented. It's as though we were part of a social club sitting around debating whether or not anyone would want to join us. Yet, we are here.

- Sergio Lebid: @Walter, Agreed!

- Adriano Autino: @Sergio, we have to be realistic, we are the only ones giving a hope, while all the 'leaders' are just preparing people to the big holocaust

- Rob Hunt: if I was Joe Public, I'd want t know *exactly* how my taxes/investment was going to benefit me

- Sergio Lebid: @Adriano, I agree, but we must push inspiration, the facts of the world ending are nebulous...

- Rob Hunt: @Adriano - gosh, you sound very negative about our future (with respect)

- Jesús Raygoza: @sjl008 - - Sure!! (by the way, what is your name?)

- Keith Henson: I happen to think that a long buildup of space industry using extra terrestrial materials won't happen before full scale nanotechnology comes along. But I think it is possible to get the cost to GEO down far enough to build power satellites that way. but that's the result of several years work on the problem.

- Adriano Autino: ok, somebody was scared by my presentation yesterday?

- G B Leatherwood: @Rob: "a round- table 'think tank' with pens and butvhers paper suggests itself to me" LOL! That's exactly what we're having! What is now needed is to collate what's been said and priortize to see what rises to the top for a plan of action. For that we need a leader for each of the three items in Issue II.

- Sergio Lebid: Sorry Jesus, con mucho gusto, Sergio Lebid

- Kim Peart: If it is real that we face crisis - then we need to identify the level of response required - as England had to in 1940

- Neda Ansari: That's what bad governments do - they rule by instilling fear in people. I lived in a world like that once. That is why revolutions are happening ;)

- Keith Henson: kim, agree

- Jesús Raygoza: I agree!! - - Adriano

- Sergio Lebid: @Neda, Yes, my experience also

- Scott Brown: We just had a thousand school children participate by inventing and preparing experiments which we shot off to sub- orbital space and then recovered the experiments and they are writing papers on the results. This is the time of real not imaginary. It is show me time, not tell me. We are no longer talking about it at Spaceport America www.spaceportamerica.com. We are doing it.

- Adriano Autino: @Neda, exactly. we have to give hope and inspiration, without denying the reality

- Stephanie Lynne Thorburn: I think that space development simply needs to be on the agenda as a credible idea for human evolution. In a way, the SRI might measure their achievement simply in terms of changing public perceptions and encouraging existing space related organisations and government agencies of our values. The SRI maybe do not have the means to carry out the plans suggested/ proposed, but there are many affiliated space organisations connecting that may be in a better position..

- Sergio Lebid: @Scott, EXCELLENT! VERY INSPIRATIONAL!

- Neda Ansari: Adriano - no one is scared here - you're a fearless leader, having us realize things on our own :)

- Sergio Lebid: @Neda, Agreed!

- Rob Hunt: @Scott, agree with Sergio 100%

- Jesús Raygoza: Sergio, ¿eres de Iberoamérica?

- Sergio Lebid: Jesus, de venezuela

- Walter C. Putnam: @Stephanie - How true. The task is to make people realize that it is another step in evolution.

- Jesús Raygoza: Neda is correct, Adriano. You are a fearless leader. Good!!

- Sergio Lebid: Jesus, pero vivo en EEUU

- Jesús Raygoza: Segio- - - Gracias.

- Sergio Lebid: Jesus, por nada

- Adriano Autino: ok, I think we had suggestions and comments to think about, and integrate in our initiative

- Sergio Lebid: Jesus, soy venezolano- ruso

- Jesús Raygoza: Sergio - - viví en USA, regresé a México para hacer unos proyectso. Después vemos.

- Neda Ansari: Sergio, are you comparing me to Jesus? Sorry I don't speak Spanish :)

- Adriano Autino: Mr. Chairman, I propose we rapidly describe each project and try to reach a conclusion for today

- G B Leatherwood: Uh, por favor, no comprendo Espanol

- Sergio Lebid: @Neda, You are very humorous...thank you

- Neda Ansari: You're welcome.

- Jesús Raygoza: Gail - - Do you understand Euskera? I think you do!! (well, a little).

- Sergio Lebid: @Adriano, Agreed

- Rob Hunt: @Adriano - agreed

- SpaceShaft: @Keith, I read many of your analyses and even if things were possible using the technologies you suggest the owners of such technologies have zero interests in bringing down such costs, nor would I would if I where in their shoes. However as you I too am a idealist believing that a technological open source projects can be put in place for SBSE. and waiting for industry to have a set of systems that could be implemented will not guarantee anything. Just see at Laser Motive prize, not only $800K but also all the contacts with the DOD and other companies that are not humnistic in any fashion

- G B Leatherwood: Jesus, thanks for the reminder, but I have enough trouble with English!

- Jesús Raygoza: Neda, it is very good for us to actually do a great task for the future (we have lost a generation stuck on Eart!! and it is too much to handle!!!)

- Sergio Lebid: @Gail, You are doing great Mr. Chairman, thank you!

- Sergio Lebid: @Jesus, Agreed!

- Jesús Raygoza: Gail... you are very modest!! And, very funny!!

- Kim Peart: Events in Egypt this year were totally out of the blue - should enough people awaken to the need to shift our thinking to a future beyond Earth - the world will roll over

- G B Leatherwood: All, Adriano has asked for a summary of our thoughts, so let's see if we can hold further conversation until we do that. Sort of a mid- course correction, if you will. Adriano, can you do this briefly?

- Sergio Lebid: @Kim, I disagree with you...Egypt was due to erupt for some time

- Keith Henson: SpaceShaft, the technology to do this doesn't really exist yet.

- Jesús Raygoza: Yes, Adriano, we need a summary.

- G B Leatherwood: People, BANG goes the gavel! Adriano, the floor, the rest, please hold your thoughts.

- Keith Henson: but it is fairly obvious that conventional chemical rockets simply will not do the job

- Neda Ansari: @Kim - I talked about this at ISDC, and it's in my book - the recent events in the mid- East errupted after Michael Doornbos of Evadot did an interview with me.

- Adriano Autino: many are still writing...

- Sergio Lebid: Dear all, Adriano is completely correct in many critical areas, the world unfortunately is in a very tender fragile situation so it is imperative that we as SRI send the message loudly and frequently about our mission for humanity

- Sergio Lebid: Sorry Mr. Cahirman

- Adriano Autino: ok, i am going to try summarizing what we said, and proceed ahead

- SpaceShaft: @Keith, I know that much of it does not exist, but that is not the point, right? Neither is CNT in the landscape for at least another 20 years right?
- G B Leatherwood: Friendly, Keith, Neda, please hold your comments.
- SpaceShaft: Ok
- Neda Ansari: Will do Gail.
- Adriano Autino: we are thinking to support our PR plan with three concret projects, more on the social side than on the technical one
- Adriano Autino: two of these projects are positive and inspiring: the space business lines trade- off and the virtual L1 Habitat
- Adriano Autino: one of the projects, the Civilization Risk Assessment & Management, is a serious assessment of the status of the civilization, faced to global risks
- Adriano Autino: having had Fukushima and Gulf of Mexico, i think people will not be scared by our project, being scared enough by such epochal catastrphes
- Adriano Autino: one project on three is maybe more addressed to the more mature part of the Earthlings, teh ones who reason about the future, about their children jobless, etc...
- Adriano Autino: It will be our sensitiveness to batch the emphasis on one or another project according to the public we will address
- Adriano Autino: sorry, i mean each time evaluating who we have in front
- Adriano Autino: however the concerns about being positive and inspirer were well received, and will orient us during the production of the materials (articles, books, plans, etc...)
- Adriano Autino: the above summary could be added to our final resolution, if we agree on that
- Adriano Autino: later i will propose it for voting
- G B Leatherwood: Adriano, if you are ready, Friendly, Keith, and Neda have been waiting patiently for their turn, then others.
- G B Leatherwood: Friendly, you go first.
    - SpaceShaft: pthanks, sorry for the delay, I was talking with Keith, I wonder about the projects proposed by Adriano, would they be someting interactive like an online game presenting the users

- SpaceShaft: with possible scenarios? if so we will need to get programmers and al the infrastructure.

- Kim Peart: Mr Chairman - permission to speak at some point

- G B Leatherwood: Friendly, I presume you're talking about the virtual space city?

- Adriano Autino: @Nelson, the idea is to involve universities, and make students work on the projects

- SpaceShaft: We could perhaps even try to get some famos people on that but I personally don't believe that is the approach I would go for

- Adriano Autino: @Nelson, two projects have an annexed questionnaire, that can be made online

- Adriano Autino: @Nelson, the third project will be online, allowing people to fly in absence of gravity in the center of teh hub, and walking on the peripheric ground

- SpaceShaft: Involving universities is nice, I have been trying to recruit people for quite some time and I have perhps failed in being charming, but it is not something I believe will work if there is no financial insentive

- Adriano Autino: @for financing, we will address foundations

- G B Leatherwood: Moving right along, Keith was next. Keith?

- Adriano Autino: this will be the Space Renaissance projects, they will listen to us

- SpaceShaft: however, I invite you to sheck out the http://eusec.warr.de website. I have been able to get some students and universities interested but there had to be a prize

- Keith Henson: you want me to say something?

- G B Leatherwood: Keith, not necessarily, but you were next in line. OK, Neda?

- Adriano Autino: of course, prizes are key, that's why we need foudnations

- SpaceShaft: and if a team (heroes) we support can be used to inspire others perhaps we should go that way

- SpaceShaft: Ok

- Neda Ansari: Translating SBSP is on my priority list - next, concentrating on talking with schools, as I've been starting space clubs in my local area. Any funding will be welcome, as I intend to make this an exclusive SRI project.

- Keith Henson: well, if you want my opinion, there is no cost effective way yet to get into space

- Keith Henson: and really no prospects for one, even skylon won't do it

- Keith Henson: that is no widely recognized way.

- Adriano Autino: thank you Keith! this is optimistic and inspiring enough! :D

- Sergio Lebid: @Keith, within 5- 7 years there will be

- G B Leatherwood: Keith, you're right, but SRI isn't the one to make that happen.

- Walter C. Putnam: @Keith - Until compared with the costs of NOT going into space

- G B Leatherwood: Kim, you wanted in. Go.

- Stephanie Lynne Thorburn: Some of the many 90 organisations that are already connected to the SRI might well be able to suggest ideas to into fruition the 2011- 15 proposed plans and/ or practical funding.

- Kim Peart: All keen on the virtual world project could agree to form a working group - communicate via Email, Skype and in the virtual world - there are over 130 of them - and return with regular reports to SRI

- Keith Henson: beamed energy is an approach, but it just won't work on a starter scale.

- SpaceShaft: @keith; you are right for current technologies and how things are commercialized, but inspiration the SRI can provide to future generations is to look for a different way to commercialize the service. The thing will ultimatelly be not for the money but for humanistic values, right?

- Adriano Autino: @Nelson, agree

- Sergio Lebid: @Nelson, You are correct

- G B Leatherwood: Thank you, Kim. The beauty of this somewhat clumsy format is that there is a written record so all the ideas can be collected and acted upon.

- Kim Peart: Anyone interested in an SRI virtual world working group - please contact me
- SpaceShaft: thanks, but thanks to Adriano primarilly because he is the one whom has publically been advocating for it since a long time
- Kim Peart: kimpeart@iinet.net.au
- Keith Henson: well, eventually nanotechnology will cut the cost of getting into space by materials improvement
- Stephanie Lynne Thorburn: The SRI might also create links to significant high- profile space- related websites and post info on proposed projects via reciprocal links..
- Krahazik Dragon: I am in with Kim on the virtual world idea.
- Keith Henson: but that will probably be too late
- Adriano Autino: @Kim, sorry, but it should be made in a more structured way, it will be an offical SRI team
- Sergio Lebid: @Keith, CORRECT!
- SpaceShaft: keith, have you looked at what I been proposing for some time already?
- Keith Henson: if you want to do it sooner, it's going to be expensive to set up
- SpaceShaft: http://spaceshaft.org
- Sergio Lebid: @Keith, not necessarily
- Keith Henson: space elevator?

[19.35.42] Voting on Issue II

- G B Leatherwood: We still have some time, but it appears that we are ready to say whether we as a group accept, approve of, and will support the three projects stated in Issue II- - but not necessarilly in the order stated. Do I hear a motion to accept?
- SpaceShaft: by going that way it will be possible to go in smaller steps, that couls finance other developments.
- Krahazik Dragon: Accept
- Sergio Lebid: @Gail, I mention
- Sergio Lebid: motion that is
- Krahazik Dragon: Kim I sent a request to add you to my skyp list.

- SpaceShaft: is something like a space elevator but is not the centrifugally extended CNT SE by Edwards
- G B Leatherwood: It has been moved that this group accept Issue II, is there a second?
- Keith Henson: ok
- Rob Hunt: I move to accept
- Walter C. Putnam: second the motion
- Rob Hunt: second
- Krahazik Dragon: second
- Neda Ansari: second
- Sergio Lebid: second
- Kim Peart: Just crashed out of Skype and climbed back in - Sure Adriano - I work within structure and report back - honesty is my policy - let's start the ball rolling and make it so
- SpaceShaft: FYI the guys at the ISEC don't wanted me to participate at the games because my system is not based on their pre- conditions
- Krahazik Dragon: Kim I sent an add request in skype.
- Anton Volkonskiy: second
- SpaceShaft: second
- Jesús Raygoza: Second
- Stephanie Lynne Thorburn: I think the proposals admirable, but would not guarantee that they could definitely be brought into fruition. V. good initiative though Adriano and thanks for the presentation and hard work on the working documents & proposals.
- Kim Peart: Thanks Dragon - can see
- G B Leatherwood: It has been moved and seconded that this group accept Issue II, is there any further discussion?
- Adriano Autino:

> We are planning to support our PR plan with three concret projects, more on the social side than on the technical one.
>
> Two of these projects are positive and inspiring: the space business lines trade- off and the virtual L1 Habitat.
>
> One of the projects, the Civilization Risk Assessment & Management, is a serious assessment of the status of the civilization,

71

faced to global risks. Having had Fukushima and Gulf of Mexico, people will not be scared by our project, being scared enough by such epochal catastrophes.

One project on three is more addressed to the more mature part of the Earthlings, teh ones who reason about the future, about their children jobless, etc...

It will be our sensitiveness to batch the emphasis on one or another project according to the public we will address, each time evaluating who we have in front.

However the concerns about being positive and inspirer were well received, and will orient us during the production of the materials (articles, books, plans, etc...)

- Fred Becker: @Adriano...whenever we bring forward a problem, we should also provide our solution. That is a good rule for avoiding fear and instilling confidence. (It is a rule used in the army).

- Adriano Autino: Mr. Chairman, if accepted by the congress, I will add the above text (duly revised) in our final resolution.

- Fred Becker: Change "inspirer" to "inspiring"?

- Sergio Lebid: Mr. Chairman, please advise if we are in an open forum position yet

- Adriano Autino: of course English shall be revised

- G B Leatherwood: Sergio, we are still open for discussion on the motion only. Waiting for a call for the vote.

- Rob Hunt: still not happy with references to specific disasters - appears shallow, popularist and alarming

- Sergio Lebid: Thank you Mr. Chairman

- Sergio Lebid: I move that call for a vote

- James Greeson: @ wheatshaeaf: it works for politicans. ;)

- Adriano Autino: I move to approve the Issue II, with the integration of the text just proposed (duly revised)

- Stephanie Lynne Thorburn: @Rob Hunt. References to specific events may however be necessary to illustrate a point- although positivity is a good policy rather than being alarmist regarding the future.

- Sergio Lebid: I motion to accept the Issue II

- Rob Hunt: @James - I thin k we're trying to be better than politicians

- Dr. Feng Hsu: @james, is SRI more of a political or philosophic org than a space technical org?

- James Greeson: at manipulating, I'm sorry, Influencing public opinion?

- G B Leatherwood: It has been moved and seconded that this group accept Issue II. It has been further amplified that the text provided by Adriano in his remarks be included. The vote has been called, all in favor signify by writing "Aye," those opposed, "Nay."

- Sergio Lebid: Aye

- James Greeson: aye

- Walter C. Putnam: @Rob - It should be understood that the list is neither definite or all inclusive.

- Anton Volkonskiy: aye

- Walter C. Putnam: Aye

- Krahazik Dragon: Aye

- SpaceShaft: Aye

- Rob Hunt: aye

- Neda Ansari: aye

- Dr. Feng Hsu: aye

- Jennifer Bolton: aye

- Kim Peart: YES

- Jesús Raygoza: AYE

- Stephanie Lynne Thorburn: Yes. I think that some of today's feedback does though, need to be taken into account.

- Dr. Feng Hsu: @james, there is good politics or bad politics.....the urgly reality on earth is that politics or politicians DO CONTROL and DOMINATE EVERYTHING..!!

- Sergio Lebid: Adriano, Mr. Chairman and All, may I make request that we establish a PR Campaign Committee?

- Adriano Autino: I was just going to say something about the organizational issues

- Dr. Feng Hsu: excellent suggestion Sergio

- Jesús Raygoza: Very good, Dr. Feng. Besides, politicians actually, rarely are right!

- G B Leatherwood: I don't know what Mr. Robers would say about procedures for an on-line voting process, but seeing no "Nay" votes I declare that Issue II passed with no dissenting votes, making it unanimous among those voting. Voting is closed, motion passed.

[19.51.11] Adjourning

Day 3 – July 9th 2011

[17.00.02] Congress Day 3 – election of the chairperson
Kim Peart is elected as chairperson (Gail Leatherwood is absent).

[17.26.47] Agenda of Day 3 and Day 4
- Adriano Autino: CONGRESS DAY 3 - Saturday July 9th 2011
15.00 GMT
  a) chairperson, if none objection => Gail
  b) approval of agenda
15.15 GMT
  c) FINAL RESOLUTION, including:
   - Political guidelines emerging from the congress, for our public outreach viral campaign
   - Congress vote on the final resolution
17.00 GMT
  d) THREE PROJECTS: titles, structure and general plans, committees, meetings
   - Congress vote on titles and chairpersons (when available)
   - Committees composition doesn't need the vote of the congress
18.00 GMT
  f) adjourn

- Adriano Autino: the angenda of tomorrow will be all on organizational matters

- Adriano Autino: CONGRESS DAY 4 - Sunday July 10th 2011
15.00 GMT
    a) chairperson, if none objection => Gail
    b) approval of agenda
15.15 GMT
    c) SRI FINANCIAL BALANCE, July 2010 - July 2011
    - Congress vote on the balance
15.45 GMT
    d) SRI EXECUTIVE COMMITTEE, including:
    - list of members
    - methodology and rules
    - main goals of the Committee, 2011 - 2015
    - Congress vote on the list of members, methodology and rules
17.30 GMT
    e) PR COMMITTEE, including:
    - general planning
    - main communication campaigns
    - new version of the SRI mission statement
    - Congress vote on setup and general planning
    - Committee composition doesn't need the vote of the congress
18.00 GMT
    g) adjourn

Agendas are approved.

[17.36.28] The Final Resolution report, by AA (part 1)
- Adriano Autino:
i would propose to download the final resolution draft... ok, let's start then
my final resolution draft was a hard work
only yesterday morning i waked up knowing what i had to write

it took me the whole day, and Kim was so kind to edit the text at the light speed...

therefore i hope you will forgive any incoherence that might be still present

i think however we did our best to catch and integrate the comments we had during teh first two days

the resolution is made of three parts:

1. Summarizing the achievements of the SRI First Congress

2. Political guidelines emerging from the congress, for our public outreach viral campaign

3. The three projects, to balance our communication

so, part 1.

Approaching the conclusion of our first international congress, we can say that our tenacity and patience, to hold this congress, though just online, was prized, in terms of participation and high quality of the discussion we had.

Such a high level of discussion allowed us to get several relevant achievements, in theory and in practice, with some new organizational structures, which began to work in these two weeks, even before the congress was completed!

we were right to decide to hold this congress, that takes place in a very critical moment, while the Space Shuttle is making its last flight

and many commenters say this is a milestone, the end of an age

i think our congress centered the matter, and we are on the edge of events, indeed!

In summary, we were able to identify some key items, to be addressed in our outreach communication effort:

1. fighting the abysmal lack of knowledge and continuing misinformation around the most promising space industrial developments, such as Space Tourism and SBSP

about that, this morning a nice (provocative) title came to my mind: space tourists? no, we want to go to space to stay!

i think we should issue our next press release on that...

second key item...

2. bringing some rather neglected space topics to the public attention, such as space debris, human life and health protection against hard radiation in space and low/zero gravity, astrobiology in general, exoagricolture and exo- farming, Near Earth Asteroids capture and mining, all topics very relevant for a serious space settlement plan

so, we have a number of topics which are very relevant for space settlement, that so far were not considered important enough, sicne the strategy was _not_ space stllement, but just science and exploration

in days 1 an 2 we discussed this aspect, and i think it is very relevant for our outreach and campaigns

3. enhancing the public awareness about the global civilization risk, paying special attention to the communication methods, and always associating this argument with our message of hope, pointing out that this is a growth crisis for our civilization, while the birth of a Civilization spanning the Solar System is approaching

we'll see in details later this point, that's a very key one

4. bringing a wind of innovation in the political / ideological environment, with our proposal to replace the obsolete ideologies of liberalism and socialism by astronautic humanism, based on compassion, exodevelopment, assuring abundance of resources for free and democratic civil development

this is very important too... in the post industrial world people is enough of teh current corrupted and cultural ignorant political leaderships

we have to propose another ideology, based on quality, no more on the old ideological memes

5. running a visionary project, the Virtual Orbital Space Settlement, that will be able to catch the imagination and raise hope in the future into the true heritage of humanity: the children of the Earth

6. running two other projects, the Civilization Risk Assessment & Management and spotting the Best Space Business Industrial Development, to engage researchers, universities and students in the urgent needs of our civilization, to step over the current global crisis and finally aiming high again

the above are the 6 main achivements of our congress, and will be our track, during the next four years with the proposal to raise public and private investments in the new spce industry

the congress also allowed us to make some essential organizational improvements, giving birth to two very important committees:

the SRI Executive Committee, that for the first time in our still brief history, can become the true direction for our international association

the SRI Public Relations Committee, that is already drawing its Plan, and in these days sent our first Press Release to a relevant number of media and agencies

Walt Putnam couldn't be with us today, but he made a great work, sending our press release for the first time to a big number of media

The large interest arised from our congress inspired many new supporters to join us, especially from the South East regions, such as India, Nepal, Malaysia, and others. The founding nucleus of the SRI India Chapter has been born,

yes, Camilo, and Rijendra, we hope you will be the first ranks of the SRI members in the emerging countries, that are manifesting an incredible enthusiams for space and astronautics!!!

just few more points, then we can make a first pause for comments

After this congress, the SRI is stronger then before, and this is not to be measured only by membership and active support, but also in our increased capacity to agree on methodologies and to take initiatives in a team spirit.

And maybe it is not a case that we are celebrating our first congress while the Shuttle Atlantis is flying for the last time. As many newspapers are writing, this the end of an age: the age of space used for Earth.

And a new age is beginning: the age of the space used for human development outside Earth, or exo- development.

   The age of Space Renaissance

what we are saying. the past 40 years space was used mostly to support the Earth's business (telecommunication)

now the age of exo- development is beginning

we have to addrees the outer space, and settle overthere

[18.17.04] The Final Resolution report (part 1) - open discussion

- Kim Peart: Open for comments

- Kim Peart: Thanks Adriano - much work

- Jesús Raygoza: Friends. Suddenly, I have to lave for a while. To come back soon, I will do as much as I can do. In case I cannot come back on time. Tomorrow, it will be possible to stay with you. Thanks!

- Rob Hunt: very good AA. As Peter Diamandis said in a TED talk a few years ago, there are 3 motivations for space development: 1. curiosity 2. fear of global disasters 3. profit. All three can be addressed by SRI philosophy

- Kim Peart: Thanks Jesus

- Adriano Autino: yes Rob. You hit the point!

- Adriano Autino: Ciao Jesus, i hope you can be back

- Anton Volkonskiy: The most important is to develop new kind of engine/propulsion

- Krahazik Dragon: agreed Anton

- Camilo Andres Reyes: I agree with digger

- Rijendra Thapa: Yeah i very much agree with Rob

- Anton Volkonskiy: chemical engine will not let us enough ...

- Rob Hunt: agreed anton, but at the same time we must create and maintain a momentum of interest in the publics mind. curiosity, fear, profit

- Camilo Andres Reyes: i think while we still using the same propulsion system is complicated to get beyond

- Adriano Autino: the mission of SRI is to raise the public awareness about the urgence of the exo- development

- Adriano Autino: it doesn't need to invent quite new technologies... do you remember X33?

- Adriano Autino: it was a concentrate of sci- fi technologies, it costed billions, and never fllew

- Adriano Autino: it was retired by NASA in 2001 (if i remember well)

- Camilo Andres Reyes: ohh ok ok

- Adriano Autino: i think SpaceComposites, SpaceX, and others, are working woth existent and almost existent technologies

- Adriano Autino: and our task is to support their efforts...

- CommanderCatalina: http://www.facebook.com/event.php?eid=185973411459145 if you are on facebook attend this webinar, Aerojet will be building an ion propulsion engine

- Adriano Autino: showing to the people that they have an high social role, not just for their profit...

- Camilo Andres Reyes: thanks for the site commander :)

- Rob Hunt: I had a thought for our PR committee...

- Adriano Autino: this generation of space entrepreneur, are our social reference...

- Rijendra Thapa: yeah i agree this may be the better way to make people more interested Adriano

- Adriano Autino: they work for profit, but they also have an ethical concept of enterprise

- Kim Peart: Yes Rob

- Rob Hunt: a simple thing occurred to me, that we might engage in supporting such things as sci- fi popular media such as star trek movies by petitioning them to continue production.

- Adriano Autino: @Rob, an excellent idea!

- Adriano Autino: it's esy to raise cause on facebook

- Neda Ansari: I sat with chief engineers from Aerojet at the last ISDC Governors Gala while we talked about ion propulsion - Beigelow was talking about the same. IP seems to be the trend these days.

- Rob Hunt: it would just add to the weight of opinion in the public's mind, keep the idealistic notions out there amongst them

- Sergio Lebid: Great idea Rob! I am in the process of securing one of the Star Trek actors who happens to be very enlightened and a PhD to join us and promote our efforts. She is a wonderful person!

- Kim Peart: Rob - as sets are built - we can make documentaries and movie stories in Second Life too

- Rob Hunt: @serg - cool

- Camilo Andres Reyes: wow, it's great....it's a wonderfull idea

- Rob Hunt: @kim - yep

- Adriano Autino: just one recomendation: any public action we begin, please sign it as Space Renaissance International! (we have to be everywhere)
- Rob Hunt: @adriano - absolutely agree
- Sergio Lebid: Definitely Adriano!
- Kim Peart: That would be fantastic Sergio
- Camilo Andres Reyes: agree
- Neda Ansari: Sergio, what's the name?
- Sergio Lebid: I should know in the next week.
- Sergio Lebid: Neda, I will advise with her permission after we are in mutual agreement.
- Adriano Autino: we have the message from Keith, i think it is pertinent with this discussion

    want to see it?
- Sergio Lebid: yes
- Rijendra Thapa: yeah
- Camilo Andres Reyes: yes
- Adriano Autino:

    Keith Henson's address

    This is something that has not been covered by news nor (as near as I can tell) has it been the subject of a press release. But it is fairly well known to those in the business.

    NASA Ames brought a 1.2 MW, 110 GHz gyrotron for testing beamed energy propulsion. They still need the power supply, which is 70 kV at 30 A but it's a relatively small cost compared to the gyrotraon. Up close it will provide well over 10 MW/m2.to test hydrogen heaters.

    They intend to offer the use o it the same way as the wind tunnels, as a national engineering test asset.

    I think it is an accepted truth that you need single stage to orbit and that it must be a reusable launch vehicle to get the cost to GEO down to where power satellites make sense economically.

Given the current state of material science and the best exhaust velocity you can get from chemical propulsion, neither of these are feasible.

To put numbers on the problem, it takes 9000 m/s to get into LEO. For 4500 m/s rocket engines, that's a delta V of twice the exhaust velocity. The rocket equation gives a mass ration of 7.4 which means the vehicle and payload can't be more than 13.5% of the takeoff mass. For a vehicle to be reusable, the accepted minimum structure is 15%, leaving less than zero for payload. (Skylon cheats by burning air partway up, but it's not enough to get a lot of payload to LEO.)

But if you have 9000 m/s exhaust velocity, which can be done with hydrogen heated with microwaves or lasers, then the mass ratio is a little less than 3. So vehicle and payload can be 36% of takeoff mass. If half vehicle and half payload, that's 18% each. So a 300 ton vehicle with a dry mass of 54 tons could put 54 tons in LEO.

The falling cost of microwave power and laser power makes these options possible.

Beamed energy propulsion doesn't make economic sense unless you are talking cargo volumes in the hundreds of thousands of tons per year.

I should also add that I never thought NASA would do something so sensible. Those of you who know Pete Warden might send him a thank you note..

Keith Henson

- Rob Hunt: @serg - nice work
- Kim Peart: Definitely
- Sergio Lebid: Thanks Rob, we are all for one and one for all at SRI!
- Krahazik Dragon: could establish branch or sattalite offices in popular virtual worlds as an extension to the outreach and RP process
- Neda Ansari: Sounds good Sergio - & that is wonderful if she could join.
- Camilo Andres Reyes: wait a minute plzz

- Sergio Lebid: Thanks Neda
- Rob Hunt: another idea for PR...
- Camilo Andres Reyes: ok
- Adriano Autino: we'll put the Keith's message in the acta of the congress, and keep it as material for our further elaboration and outreach
- Sergio Lebid: agreed
- Camilo Andres Reyes: agree
- Adriano Autino: all the ideas proposed here should be conveied to the PR Committee
- Sergio Lebid: agreed
- C.A. Chicoine: Hello, I've been reading from the side-lines. :) I'd like to comment on what Rob brought up regarding sci-fi and popular media. Perhaps a coalition of writers could be formed with the conscious effort to promote SRI?
- Adriano Autino: C.A. that would be great!
- Kim Peart: Adriano - as Keith suggests - if we know Pete Warden - SRI could contact him
- Camilo Andres Reyes: but is it possible??
- Xavier Alabart: I will suggest going via Gary Martin which also is at NASA Ames, he tends to be very open minded
- Rob Hunt: merchandising - I go to lots of meetings for many astro societies etc and talks to the public. SRI stickers/merchandise would be good to distribute -
- Adriano Autino: C.A., are you already in the PR Committee?
- Rijendra Thapa: rob has a nice point
- C.A. Chicoine: Adriano, no I am not on a committee.
- Kim Peart: Cachicoine - Excellent thought - the Second Life SRI movie house could go viral
- Sergio Lebid: Great idea Rob
- Adriano Autino: C.A. will you accept to join the SRI PR Committee?
- Rob Hunt: @kim and others - second life SRI brilliant idea
- C.A. Chicoine: Yes. :)
- Adriano Autino: excelletnt!

- Kim Peart: Welcome
- Sergio Lebid: Great
- Adriano Autino: Rob, you are in the PR Committee, right?
- Camilo Andres Reyes: WOW
- Rob Hunt: me??? no, no experience at all
- Adriano Autino: ok, but you have ideas, man!
- Rob Hunt: ideas are the easy part
- Adriano Autino: so please join the committee :)
- Sergio Lebid: Rob, you great ideas qualify you!
- Sergio Lebid: your
- Rijendra Thapa: Sergio
- Rijendra Thapa: i agree with u
- Rob Hunt: I suffer from lack of self confidence having only *very* recently come to the astro/space sector later in life. I doubt my own abilities.
- CommanderCatalina: pete.worden@nasa.gov
- Sergio Lebid: Rob, we do not doubt your abilities and we will help each other learn and grow and progress!
- Adriano Autino: Rob, don't be shy, the committee is learning how to develop the SRI outreach...
- Krahazik Dragon: I have doupts baout my own participation and worth
- Adriano Autino: we have professionals in it
- Camilo Andres Reyes: we can help each other
- Rob Hunt: OK, you asked for it! I'm in, thankyou.
- Adriano Autino: great! -
- Sergio Lebid: Great!
- Kim Peart: Welcome Rob
- Rob Hunt: tnx kim
- Adriano Autino: well, i am marking the action items, that will be easier to find them...
- Adriano Autino: I think we can proceed, mr. chairman, or will come too late...

- Rob Hunt: brb
- Kim Peart: Yes Adriano - the next item
- Camilo Andres Reyes: YES

[18.44.43] The Final Resolution report (part 2)

- Adriano Autino:

2. Political guidelines emerging from the congress, for our public outreach viral campaign

so the first poilitical guideline is fighting misinformation

i will go through the main points as quick as i can

The privatization of space - key to open the high frontier

We keep on reading and observing in the media, superficial and misleading opinions about space tourism.

According to these views, space tourism would be a kind of very expensive amusement for rich people. Some of these opinions charge space tourism with immorality in a time of crisis, as a waste of money and valuable resources.

Since we don't only talk inside the space community, we shall develop a wide popular campaign, against such positions, focusing on commonsense with public opinion, the key elements of which are the following.

I think you all know here the young history of space tourism

yes i am talking about history, and not pre- history, neither sci- fi

history begins in 1996, with the x- prize, made by Diamandis and Mariniak (no need to explain, i think)

in 2004, ScaledComposites won the game, and changed the paradigm

Burt Rutan and Jim Benson demonstrated that they can develop a spacecraft, two stages both recoverable, with less than 30 million

yes, it is a suborbital, of course

but it retakes the path interrupted when the X15 project was canceled by NASA, in favour of Space Shuttle and spendable rockets

I guess the youngs among us could be listening for the first time to our reconstruction of the history of astronautics, and to our criticism to the space policiy

this is something we at SRI, and before, we discuss since at least 10 years

and a large literature can be found on the SRI website, and on Space-Future.com

however, back to the point, SpaceShipOne demonstrated that the low cost access to space is feasible

and triggered the crisis of the big agencies

just one flight of the shuttle costs 500 million...

privatization is the key word

SpaceX, Bigelow, Virgin Galactic are following that path

When we wrote our book "Three Theses for the Space Renaissance", the number of companies in the new space industry has grown by one magnitude, from 20 companies in 2004 to more than 100 and some of them (Virgin galactic) are well positioned to develop the suborbital tourism industry. Others, such as Bigelow and

SpaceX, aim directly for the Earth Orbit market, developing inflatable hotel accommodation and low cost orbital vehicles.

our key point, to be repeated each time we have the possibility:

Space Tourism, starting at suborbital and progressing to orbital, is the business segment that can progressively grow, accumulating capital for progressively improving the technologies, until a fully Reusable Launch Vehicle is achieved.

it means that ST, if there where time enough, could open the frontier alone, with the sole power of the growing market.

growing the market, the price of tickets will decrease, and boost the market as a feedback effect

but there's not time enough

this awful crisis menaces to crash the gloabl economy and kill any hope to go anywhere

that's why we call for the help of the politics

and we do not reject the government support

for that we need to raise the public awareness

Second theme

Space Based Solar Power - key to the Space Development

If Space Tourism is the preferred ideological target of backward- thinking anti- capitalist ideologists, SBSP is the preferred target of vested interests in oil and other well- entrenched energy lobbies.

Keith, there are market studies giving high projections to ST

a market of 1 trillion / year in few years, when it will really take off

ST will become the first industrial development line, in the globalized economy

please check spacefuture.com Patrick Collins's papers

this is the longest part of the report, i have to go streight ahead

however, SpaceShipTwo should be ready to start flying, nowadays, we will see

so, we were beginning the SBSP point

there are many false perceptions to be demistified

Energy beams from space have been the subject of endless conspiracy theories and withering scrutiny, despite a 2009 NASA study that concluded microwaves from space would be slightly less intense than the Sun's rays and would pose no danger to people.

We discussed, during day 1 and day 2, the danger that SBSP could be just a new Earthly space business, as telecommunication satellites were for the past 40 years

just relaunching the spendable rockets, instead of developing RLVs

Dr. Feng Hsu argumented it is not possible

since SBSP needs RLV, to develop

it could never be financially competitive using spendable rockets

The earthly photovoltaic industry stays on the market only because of government incentives: when the money runs out, such industries fail and many people are jobless again.

In the energy field, nothing is financed if it was never done before

We also need to consider how to promote SBSP, where there is an immense quantity of technical and engineering work to be done. People tend to undervalue the effort required. Consider that nothing has been sent into orbit, so far, in the field of energy and nobody funds anything that is not already demonstrated as a working option...

Considering the very huge effort still to be made to fly demonstrators and then building the first operative plants, this is still mainly a matter for governments and international cooperation.

After throwing so much public money out the window (absurd military expense, just for an example), this would be a very worthwhile use of public funding.

Having achieved the low cost access to orbit, establishing space based solar plants is the logical next step, in the direction of exo- industry development.

We should make it definitely clear, that the space solar plants are indispensable to all space development in the Geo- Lunar space region.

The SBSP stations will fuel hotels, industrial orbiting platforms, and ion- propulsion passenger and cargo vehicles for any destination.

Without SBSP, no exo- development program can happen.

If directed to Earth rectennas, the SBSP energy will also contribute to solve the energy problems on Earth, though this may not be the main goal.

Our vision is strongly projected outward and upward, and shall be communicated everywhere, always countering any Earth- centric view that would confine SBSP to Earth use alone.

what we have to start thinking, is outside

this is the main philosophical effort, of the SRI

go over the pre- copernican vision of the world

think about a greather house, over the Moon orbit, including the Earth magnetosphere, at least

that includes the Lagrange points as well, and many many NEAs...

always refer to that environment, at least

likely we are not yet able to think ourselves in the Mars orbit, yet

maybe our nephew will be

however, to settle in the Greater Earth, we do need Solar Power Space Plants

definitely

I call it exo- development, retaking a terminology initiated by Krafft Ehricke in his papers "The Extraterrestrial Imperative"

Few words to explain the meaning of the term 'exo- development'. We could use 'space development', and maybe within our community it would be clear enough, but I think exo- development is more appropriate: when people will ask what we mean, we will have a chance to develop our discourse.

'Exo- development' means human industrial development out of Earth, while the term 'space development' was used traditionally for any space business, including the telecommunication satellites during the 40 years of use of space for Earth.

Exo- development means use space for human development outside Earth, the new strategy, as Jeff Greason indicated clearly. According to David Dunlop, NSS is talking about bootstrapping the exo- development too.

enovironment is not just Earth's surface, but also the orbit, the Moon, the asteroids...

we have to learn mastering such environment, and take care of it, as we shall do with earth

moving our development outside, we will help Earth to recover from the burden of our development

@Stephanie, I also know that our message is for many aspects against the current, and our duty is to explain it as better as we can, not to follow the current

the current policy and philosophy led the civilization into the current awful situation

i am not saying we should not support the use of SBSP for Earth...

but we shall always recall that its main use is for the space

2.2. Raising public attention on some disciplines essential for Space Development

i'll just cover the titles of this section, i think there will not be much to discuss

2.2.1. Space debris

6000 tonns of debris are a danger for increasing astroanutic flights

and are a huge richness (about 120 billions) that could be partially re-used, instead of being burned in the athmposphere

2.2.2. Human life and health protection against space hard radiations and low/zero gravity

if we are serious with a space settlement plan, these disciplines shall be boosted, as all exo-biology, exo-agriculture, exo-farming

2.2.3. Near Earth Asteroids capture and mining

the delta V needed to reach some NEAs is surprisingly low

easier than what people thinks, we shall say it, and argument it

NEA mining could be earlier that what people think, and boost the construction of space infrastructure

2.3. Heralding a new breeze of innovation in the political / ideological environment

here i have to spend few more words

As we wrote in our Issue I for this congress, we keep on voting for collectivist or liberist utopias, but we are expected to be satisfied by real socialism and real liberalism, both of which have famously failed, as demonstrated by a long series of terrible catastrophes. The current political leaderships of our globalized society are demonstrably inadequate to the challenges now being faced.

We said we want to replace those obsolete ideologies – that have repeatedly demonstrated their tragic inadequacy – with a brand new ideology: astronautic humanism, based on compassion for all humans and for all the sentient beings.

Basing on a virtually infinite resources platform, AH is the sole ideology that can propose a feasible utopia

to develop a Solar Civilization of thousand trillions human beings, a wide free market of thousands trillions, a multicultural society based on millions of communities, each one developing their preferred values and cultural diversification, able to exchange their experiences and achievements, toward a true human status, though bodies shapes and physiologies will of course progressively differ.

Counting on the trillions comets made of ice and basic life components, and orbiting around our Solar System in the immense Oort Cloud, our offspring will never die of starvation or thirst.

will never seek to impose any "ideal social model" to anybody, since the immense resources of the Solar System, the Kuiper Belt and the Oort Cloud, will allow an endless democratic revolution, and the conditions of scarcity of resources that favour the growth of bureaucratic powers will never rise again in human history.

it means all communities will be free, for the first time in history, to develop their preferred social model

The history of the past demonstrates that, more than the social model, the moral qualities of the leaders are highly relevant in human communities and national governance.

Orbiting cities and islands in space will favour self- government and direct democracy, much more than large nations. It could be in space communities that humans will find again, in another environmental dimension, the human sized relationships, where each one is appreciated and respected for their abilities.

a social environment in which each one can aim and get what their imagination can conceive and where the people with less imagination will not need to be angry and jealous, since the general abundance of resources will allow everybody to share everything.

That kind of society is likely the nearest thing to a society where people will have the realization of their own happiness.

the above is just the tentative to start going over those few words: replacing the obsolete ideologies

is just a seed

think about evolution of the concepts...

in a context of endless abundant of resources...

ok, going to the end

2.4. Is this the end or the beginning of the space age?

On June 30th The Economist published an article titled "The end of the Space Age: Inner space is useful. Outer space is history", www.economist.com/node/18897425.

that article sounds particularly insulting for astronautic humanists...

The article postulates simply that, with the last flight of space shuttle Atlantis, the space age has ended.

"Space tourism" says the article "is a luxury service that is, in any case, unlikely to go beyond low- Earth orbit at best (the cost of getting even as far as the moon would reduce the number of potential clients to a handful).

The other source of revenue is ferrying astronauts to the benighted International Space Station (ISS), surely the biggest waste of money, at $100 billion and counting, that has ever been built in the name of science."

The article also says that space - - the inner space, inside Earth Orbit – worked greatly for Earth business during the last 40 years: exactly as we say in our analysis: the satellite age was excellent for earthly business, but not for astronautics and not for the advancement of human civilization!

How to answer to lobbyists and ideological adversaries?

One of our main tasks is: how to answer the Economist.

should we try to answer just on the basis of the Earth business, we would fail

If we want to be effective, and catch the people's attention, showing the cultural ignorance of the economist's approach to global problems, we have to use our analysis of the Civilization global risk.

It was said, in our discussion: "despite the end of world forecasts of the catastrophists, the world is always spinning around in the cosmos". It was also proposed that we should point out more of the positive aspects of our proposals, in order not to scare people.

However, we shall consider (see the book "Three Theses for the Space Renaissance", chapter "The Status of Civilization") that we are living in unprecedented times, characterized by the global extension of several social and physical processes:

- the world never had seven billions inhabitants before

- the world was never 70% industrialized

- the world never had before repeated default of countries, such as Argentina, Ireland, Greece, Portugal, …

- the world has never before had a rate of "apocalypse size" disasters so high, e.g. tsunamis, earthquakes, hurricanes, oil spills (Gulf of Mexico 2010), nuclear accidents following earthquake and tsunamis (Japan 2011)

the world has never before had a global economic crises like the current one, which started in 2008 and has yet to end

Other growing concerns at this time include:

- a global shortage of fish and other food resources (also due to use of agriculture for energy generation)
- a shortage of fresh water
- global pollution and decay of the human living environment
- acidification of the oceans, due to excess of CO_2 (also due to increasing use of coal by China for energy production)

Only the Space Renaissance has an explanation for the above. We call it the closed world syndrome. We are facing the incredible contradiction between a growing population, meaning potentially larger markets and at the same time a decrease of jobs!

Such contradiction can be caused only by a general shortage of resources and energy!

yes, the world reached similar conditions - - though they were never global like nowaday!—it always kept on spinning; but how? By terrible wars and blood baths

The risk of a global civilization (unrecoverable) crash is very real. This is nothing to be scared of, but a challenge that we can take on and fight against.

Astronautic humanists are dead against wars as a way to 'solve' the problems of the Earth and we have the good alternative: exo- development, in the outer space!

Nobody else promotes this analysis – except Stephen Hawking and a few others, mostly unheeded – and nobody else is proposing a global solution. We do, and shall keep on doing it, amplifying our voice many times.

the above is the main nucleus of our understanding of the civilization situation, and is our duty to find the best ways and modes to communicate it

we also have to discuss with other positions... but i'll go quickly, since they were discussed many times before this congress

2.4.2. The extreme ecologist position

Their answer to the global metaphysical warming is to hide their head in the sand, to de- industrialize the world and decrease the economy (they call themselves supporters of the "happy decrease") and pray to the nature goddess to save their lives...

another (more rare) category of ecologists, with those who include the solar system in their reflection, but just to say that we, humans, don't have the right to change the environments of the Moon or Mars and that we should leave them untouched

Of course, we will discuss such a position, since nobody lives on the Moon or Mars, except maybe some viruses and/or simple vegetable form of life.

We can argue that comets and asteroids are quite volatile components of the Solar System, including the Oort Cloud System. The comets are subject to losing most of their mass, when they come near the Sun. Having asteroids with very unsteady orbits that are often captured by Jupiter and hurled into the inner solar system.

However, our best positive way to talk about the crisis and the global risk is the metaphor of the Earth Pregnancy

that gives the awareness of the risk (stillbirth), should the world remain closed

and the hope of a very happy event: the birth of a solar civilization

well, it was hard, but this is the end

[19.54.01] Adjourning

Day 4 – July 10th 2011

[17.11.07] CONGRESS DAY 4 – ELECTION OF THE CHAIRPERSON / AGENDA APPROVAL

Gail B Leatherwood was elected as chairperson

15.15 GMT

    a) Discussion and vote on the FINAL RESOLUTION

    b) SRI FINANCIAL BALANCE, July 2010 - July 2011

    - Congress vote on the balance

15.45 GMT

    c) SRI EXECUTIVE COMMITTEE, including:

    - list of members

    - methodology and rules

    - main goals of the Committee, 2011 - 2015

- Congress vote on the list of members, methodology and rules

17.30 GMT
d) PR COMMITTEE, including:
- general planning
- main communication campaigns
- new version of the SRI mission statement
- Congress vote on setup and general planning
- Committee composition doesn't need the vote of the congress

18.00 GMT
f) adjourn

[17.19.32] Congress Day 4 – Discussion and vote the Final Resolution

- G B Leatherwood: This usually goes under the heading of "Unfinished Business" and is at the top of the agenda. We can go ahead with the discussion, then someone can move adoption, get a second, then call for the vote. Very tidy (and bureaucratic!)
- Adriano Autino: ok, so let's open for comments
- Rob Hunt: I made a few notes during Adriano's delivery yesterday - just a couple thoughts...
- G B Leatherwood: Rob, you have the floor.
- Rob Hunt: tnx. I want to repeat my caution about the 'fear' side of the campaign. I thinks it's counterproductive to make humans fear global disaster to try to get them to change their habits, so...
- Rob Hunt: I think we should be appealing to their desire to co- operatively reduce the humanities burden on the Earth
- Sergio Lebid: Agreed Rob!
- Adriano Autino: @Rob, I share your suggestion, that is the best move to mitigate the global civilization risk
- perez.saul: agree with @ Rob
- Kim Peart: This is an extremely complex issue
- Camilo Andres Reyes: agree with everyone

- Kim Peart: If the solution were simple, we would not have the problem

- Rob Hunt: @kim agreed, just don't think we should "hammer" the negative

- Angelle: Very good, Rob! Valid point.

- Sergio Lebid: Solutions are never simple or plausible without cooperation

- Rob Hunt: the stick should be used in conjunction with the carrot

- Stephanie Lynne Thorburn: I think it is a question of balance- it is not really a 'fear orientated' campaign when there have in reality been many natural disasters of late and there are a range of issues of human origin to be considered in Earth's fragile future. Sustainable development is really a reduction in humanity's burden on Earth and not radical enough as a solution. The risk assessment concept is a positive idea for conveying exo- development to the public as a viable option.

- Kim Peart: Agreed Rob - One sentence cannot explain a careful communication

- Rob Hunt: @stephanie agreed

- Sergio Lebid: Exactly Stephanie and agreed!

- Camilo Andres Reyes: i agree with stephanie

- Adriano Autino: @Rob (sorry for stoling the job of the chairman here), do you want to propose an amendment or an addition to the final resolution, or just to record a recommendation for our outreach modulation?

- G B Leatherwood: As a manager I used to say "Don't bring me problems- - I know what the problems are. Bring me solutions!"

- Rob Hunt: just wanted to express a moderating voice - the document is fine as it is

- Sergio Lebid: fear is irrelevant to a logical thought process for sustainabilty

- Rob Hunt: @gail - yes

- Rob Hunt: also....

- Sergio Lebid: Exactly Gail!

- Krahazik Dragon: Think of the solution not the problem.

- Sergio Lebid: Exactly Krahazik!

- Stephanie Lynne Thorburn: So Adriano's initiatives and the concepts contained in 'Three Project for the SRI' are constructive- as is the 'Final Resolution' document, but these plans need to be expressed carefully so that they appear plausible and a culmulative approach employed to realise these goals.

- Camilo Andres Reyes: i think we shold talk together about the problem to find together as a team the solution!!

- Adriano Autino: but we shall also demonstrate to the people that we are aware of the problems, or they will not think we are serious

- Kim Peart: We do need to be brutally honest with reality

- Adriano Autino: so, it is a balance, as Kim said, the PR Committee will have to tune our message

- Angelle: Appropriately stated, Krahazik, Stephanie and Gail !

- Kim Peart: we are no bast 150% unsustainable - a bubble that can or must burst

- Rob Hunt: @kim, agreed but use the truth as a motivator, not as a resentful blaming tool

- Sergio Lebid: Exactly Rob!

- Kim Peart: History tells us that the truth does not motivate - denial is something we do

- G B Leatherwood: Logical or not, fear is a highly powerful emotion and the general public is not always (if ever!) logical. It's the job of our PR Comm to find ways to say "Here's the problem; here's the SRI sollution."

- Rob Hunt: yup

- Camilo Andres Reyes: agree

- C.A. Chicoine: - Adriano Autino:
    <<< so, it is a balance, as Kim said, the PR Committee will have to tune our message - Agreed. :)

- Kim Peart: Our greatest threat is polite conversation that avoids addressing real causes and fails to look at real solutions

- Sergio Lebid: Yes indeed Gail but we should not dwell on fear but the postive potential outcome by doing the right thing for humanity and sustainability...

- G B Leatherwood: It seems like we are in agreement:

- Sergio Lebid: Yes gail
- Sergio Lebid: Gail
- Stephanie Lynne Thorburn: Yes, and the SRI solution should resonate as a natural developmental path for the continuation of our future.
- Camilo Andres Reyes: Steph u get the point
- Sergio Lebid: Indeed Stephanie!
- G B Leatherwood: 1. Be positive in our approach, 2. Don't be shy about the truth of the problems, 3. task the PR Comm with the job of conveying this to the public. Can we agree on that and move on?
- Sergio Lebid: Camilo, Stephanie is a leading advocate of the POINT!
- Rob Hunt: aye aye
- Kim Peart: Yes
- Sergio Lebid: Excellent Gail!
- Adriano Autino: @Stephanie, may I recommend you to prepare an address for the PR committee on this subject?
- Angelle: Agreed, Gail
- Sergio Lebid: Agreed Gail!
- Adriano Autino: @Stephanie I find your comments very much on the point
- Camilo Andres Reyes: yes, i know! ;)
- Adriano Autino: Gail, second
- Sergio Lebid: (y)
- Jesús Raygoza: One of our real best solutions is to develop high-tech (which is usually cleaner than the old) on Earth, and it is mainly done through developing technology to colonize space. This is one of my main arguments explained to a regular citizen in the world (wherever I go). Therefore, it is a stronger argument for people to understand that humans can get a cleaner planmet by developing space technology.
- Sergio Lebid: Indeed Jesus!
- Camilo Andres Reyes: rght
- Stephanie Lynne Thorburn: Many thanks all. An address on clear communication and constructive rhetoric- or the recent excellent papers by Adriano et al?
- Jesús Raygoza: Sure! Sergio.

- Sergio Lebid: I agree with you Jesus!

- Jesús Raygoza: Thank you, Sergio.

- Sergio Lebid: My pleasure

- Adriano Autino: @Stephanie, I was just proposing you to assemble your coments in this discussion, maybe add the Gail recomendation, a short address

- Rob Hunt: another observation from last night's discussion pls mr chair?

- Angelle: Stephanie, communication is paramount in the understanding by others.

- G B Leatherwood: I believe we have finished the comments on your initial comment, Rob, so go ahead. Folks, Rob has the floor. Please let him continue,

- Kim Peart: Appreciate problem - understand cause - identify solution - design plan of action - tell the story

- Jesús Raygoza: And, we are not only have a convincent work for the regular citizen or a private enterprise, we are to actually convince our national governments, as well.

- Rob Hunt: again, this doesn't affect the voting on the resolution as it is, just comment. we'll need to flesh out the definition of Astronautical Humanism, so that it's clear and credible in the public's mind

- Jesús Raygoza: Sure. We need to design plan of action, Kim.

- Rob Hunt: involve some sociologists, philosophers, economists etc

- Rob Hunt: human competativeness/greed worries me

- Sergio Lebid: Exactly Rob!

- Adriano Autino: our definition of Astronautical Humanism is on our Manifesto

- Adriano Autino: and in my book "Earth is not Sick: She's Pregnant!" (unfortunately in Italian language only)

- Rob Hunt: @adriano, yes but it's very superficial, lacks detail

- Adriano Autino: @Rob, true, the manifesto is not a book

- Adriano Autino: Stephanie is developing her academic work on it

- Sergio Lebid: Rob, Adriano's excellent work is a very stron foundation to further enhance...

- Kim Peart: Rob - we have the whole book of Nature to guide us - if we learn to read it properly
- Sergio Lebid: strong
- Camilo Andres Reyes: I like that words: ASTRONAUTICAL HUMANISM...I think we should take to all people around the world to the space...I mean, many people doesn't feel the "space program" close, as theirs
- Rob Hunt: cool
- Adriano Autino: we also have Stephen Ashworth as well...
- Sergio Lebid: Good point Kim!
- Camilo Andres Reyes: the space belong to everyone in the world
- Camilo Andres Reyes: include the smallest person
- Adriano Autino: and, in the book "Three These for the Space Renaissance" there is a whole chapter (the first one) dealing the matter
- Jesús Raygoza: You are correct, Adriano. Our planet is not sick, it is pregnant. I understand.
- Sergio Lebid: Exactly Camilo!
- perez.saul: good point Adriano
- Rob Hunt: don't like the 'pregnant' analogy, sorry
- Kim Peart: With the birth delayed, the risk is now a stillbirth
- Adriano Autino: and, the forerunners of AH were Krafft Ehrick, Gerard O'Neill, Kostantin Tsiolkowky
- Camilo Andres Reyes: pregnant? haha, that word in that sense sounds a litlle funny
- Adriano Autino: none of them had to consider a 7 billion civilization... this is where we become essential
- Adriano Autino: our elaboration, I mean
- Sergio Lebid: Exactly Adriano!
- Camilo Andres Reyes: yes adriano
- Adriano Autino: I say: we cannot be humanist if we are not astronaut
- Camilo Andres Reyes: completely agree
- Adriano Autino: and we cannot be astronaut if we are not humanist
- Camilo Andres Reyes: no

- Jesús Raygoza: It does sound a little funny, indeed, Camilo... yet, I think it is a proper way to describe it.

- Kim Peart: Rob - in terms of Nature, the birth concept is natural

- G B Leatherwood: Rob, sounds like another job for the PR Comm! How to get the concept across without it sounding like we're some kind of new kooky cult.

- Camilo Andres Reyes: @Adriano: of course we can be humanist even if we aren't astronauts

- Sergio Lebid: Agreed gail and the PR message will be very clear and affect everyone

- Adriano Autino: @Gail, yes, the most complex task: to summarize our philosophy is not easy

- Stephanie Lynne Thorburn: @Rob. Yes, the 'pregnant Earth' idea is evocative and an analogy open to a variety of interpretation- I have analysed this as part of my work on the SRI. In terms of an address on communication- here's something I prepared earlier- one of my SRI press releases on the theme of clear, credible communication. 'Efficacous Duality'- I have as ever summaries some of the recent key themes of the SRI, offered a social history of the organisation and overviewed one of Patrick Collins' papers on popular music and the media in relation to the SRI's strategic plans from 2011- 2015. This approach serves to bring together an approachable feel to the SRI as an organisation and in no way suggests a potentially marginalised group. I have begun at the inception with information on some of the man affiliate organisations of the SRI. Information- approachability- social awareness and policy are the thematics here; O'Neill and all the philosophers central to the SRI's ethos are introduced in a culmulative capacity. The idea of this PR is to engage.http://www.pr- inside.com/efficacious- duality- the- space- renaissance- brian- r2346566.htm

- Keith Henson: I know this group has little concern for practical but . . . . there are a few problems here

- Camilo Andres Reyes: @Jesús: I just said it sounded funny in that way, but of course that's the point

- Stephanie Lynne Thorburn: http://www.pr- inside.com/efficacious- duality- the- space- renaissance- brian- r2346566.htm

- Jesús Raygoza: It does not have to be acult- - - it is a real and simple scientific fact. Humans are Earth's children- - - right?

- Rob Hunt: the issue for me with the pregnant analogy is that we're saying that Earth is sick, so we're saying our pregnant life- bearer is full of bad stuff, but still we want to capitalise on the feel- good nature of pregnancy. I think the metaphor is mixed and not effective

- Camilo Andres Reyes: that's correct Jesus

- Angelle: When dealing with governments, it's imperative that "Political Correctness" is used in reference to our approach. We get one chance usually and each word used to convince them is paramount.

- Sergio Lebid: Brilliant and exactly Stephanie!!!

- G B Leatherwood: Rob, again a good point and one the PR Comm should deal with.

- Adriano Autino: @Rib, we are saying Earth is NOT Sick: She's Pregnant!

- Kim Peart: Keith - I am keen to know what you see

- Jesús Raygoza: Keith, I actually think, the concept of "Earth pregnant" is a practical issue. We are Earth's children... therefore, we can take a real and practical action to solve a probelm.

- Rob Hunt: I have one last point before I must sign off...

- Sergio Lebid: Exactly Jesus! Thank you!

- Jesús Raygoza: You are welcome, Sergio.

- G B Leatherwood: Ok, Rob, you've given us much to chew on, so lay one more on us.

- Kim Peart: Rob - if the problem is delayed birth - then we have a big problem

- Adriano Autino: we have also another effective analogy: when children are grown up, they should go outside, not keep on living on teh shoudler of their Mother!

- Adriano Autino: the best thing we can do now is to leave Mom alone, to take a breath after our quick growth!

- Camilo Andres Reyes: completely rght adriano

- CommanderCatalina: you mean out of the cradle?

- Rob Hunt: this is the Mars/Moon issue. We talk about industrialising the geo- lunar ecosphere, but there is a strong anti- moon, pro- mars lobby out there...

- Jesús Raygoza: You have said a very perfect explanation, Adriano.

- Sergio Lebid: Indeed Adriano!

- CommanderCatalina: Perhaps this is why we should the develp the tech for a lunar settlement as Jesus has explained in his paper

- Jesús Raygoza: Our best chance is precisely to go out of the cradle, Maria.

- Rob Hunt: we need to be clear that we know mars has high re- source/settlement value and can be readily reached soon after we get to the moon

- Stephanie Lynne Thorburn: @ Sergio. Thanks. My academic work is more academic, but press releases need to be that bit more engaging. I think comparative existing environmental and socio- cultural develop- mental issues are important to integrate into SRI discourse so that people can see our theory in relation to existing strands of thought and in relation to; and as more attractive.

- Sergio Lebid: I agree Stephanie and my pleasure!

- Rob Hunt: we want the Robert Zubrins of the world on- side, not off- side

- G B Leatherwood: Rob, I'm not sure we can deal with that one here. That's going to be like the arguments for/against human vs. robotic exploration- - well about our pay grade right now.

- Rob Hunt: understood...happy to drop it

- G B Leatherwood: I meant "well above" our pay grade.

- Adriano Autino: @Rob, we had this discussion however

- Adriano Autino: some Mars supporters were in the SRI at the begin- ning

- Angelle: Hear hear, Stephanie

- Adriano Autino: and they could still be around

- Sergio Lebid: Rob, we can discuss but it is not ideal for the Robert Zubrins to accept our mission...

- Rob Hunt: yes, there's so much to talk about with all these wonderful people. thanks everyone, but I have to get some sleep. happy chatting!

- Adriano Autino: we have an agenda for near future, middle term and long distant future

- Sergio Lebid: Excellent points Rob as always! have a super rest!

- G B Leatherwood: Thanks for your participation, Rob! Until next time: Ad Astra!

- Adriano Autino: we say humanity should settle some advanced posts on Mars within this centiry

- Keith Henson: I kind of suspect I am the only engineer here. I can explain, i.e., put numbers on the problems if someone wants.

- Adriano Autino: but of course before runnnig we shall learn to walk

- Kim Peart: Adriano - I see our present stage on Earth as adelescent - when I look at how our expansion beyond Earth would pan out, I see that we would become a mature and cultured star- faring society

- Camilo Andres Reyes: I'm a engineer too

- Camilo Andres Reyes: :)

- Sergio Lebid: Keith, never assume the wrong thing..only assume what you know:)

- Adriano Autino: so LEO, GEO, Moon, L1, Asteroids, Mars is a natural progression

- C.A. Chicoine: It's a matter of perspective. - - "Leaving the nest/cradle" - - The Earth being our mother. As Carl Sagan once said, "We are star- stuff". We are made from the stars. So we are part of not only the Earth, but of this solar system - - the Milky Way galaxy, etc. So, we can use any number of perspectives to help relate our cause among the masses. Using the Mother Earth scenario is one that most of us can relate to, scientist or not.

- Keith Henson: human settlement of mars is just out of the range of the possible given the current state of the art

- CommanderCatalina: we are in LEO and GEO...time for the Moon

- Angelle: Nice meeting you, Rob. Rest well. (*)

- Arthur Woods: If Earth is indeed pregnant it may be so that it can send (i.e. plant) its seeds in the cosmos in order to perpetuate life. These "seeds" may or may not include humanity.

- Adriano Autino: @Keith, agree

- Sergio Lebid: Keith, yes, of course...

- Adriano Autino: back to the first priority: RLV and low cost access to orbit

- Jesús Raygoza: You are correct, Keith. Mars still is out of the range for humans to safely reach.

- Adriano Autino: this our political immediate agenda

- Rob Hunt: happy to vote for last nights resolution as is. good night all. :)

- Camilo Andres Reyes: godd ight

- Keith Henson: camilo, what sort of engineer? I am EE but wide knowledge outside that field, particularly in space

- Camilo Andres Reyes: have a nice dreams Rob

- Kim Peart: Keith - as in Egypt this year, people with a vision for liberty can cause swift change

- Sergio Lebid: Good night Rob!

- Adriano Autino: Bye Rob, and thanks for your very useful comments

- Camilo Andres Reyes: I'm a mechanical engineering student :)

- Kim Peart: See ya Rob

- G B Leatherwood: Folks, SRI is still very much in the early stages, and as Adriano has said from the beginning SRI is a philosophical organization, and if the people don't agree, the technology won't matter. The technology will flow from a solid philosophical foundation which is what SRI is trying to establish. We'll have to rely on the engineers and scientists to enable the philosophy.

- Camilo Andres Reyes: agree with G B

- Sergio Lebid: Agreed Gail!

- Jesús Raygoza: Agree with Gail.

- Angelle: Point well put, Gail. Concur

- Adriano Autino: As Arthur pointed out, Gaia, like a big oak, needs squirrels to spread her seeds around...

   Gaia is a planet, and needs a technological species, we are her squirrels (:))

- Stephanie Lynne Thorburn: Yes, we have a clear agenda and I think that one further issue is that the SRI actually challenges social thinking on the parameters of human scientific, technological evolution. There

105

is a certain amount of cultural skepticism surrounding what is too often perceived as sci- fi space exploration concepts that have permeated into the popular consciousness in fiction, films etc in the media. We need to work on a positive ethos for the SRI's concepts- rationalisation is at the heart of my social theory of the SRI re. Max Weber. Actually, the SRI's ideas are highly rational, but could be conveyed as too ambitious or not achievable. Realising a transformational unifying vision is therefore important through communicating in a balanced and evocative mode of thought.

- G B Leatherwood: I hate to be dictatorial, but we do need to move on; we're getting farther and farther behind. Do I hear a motion to adopt Adriano's presentation as a foundation document for SRI?

- Jesús Raygoza: I agree Gail. We are to move on.

- Camilo Andres Reyes: yes, let's go on

- Scott Brown: I thought we were an action group, not just a philosophical group

- Sergio Lebid: Perfectly said and agreed Stephanie! Thank you!

- Angelle: Agreed, Gail

- Sergio Lebid: Motion to adopt Adriano's presentation

- perez.saul: we need to present our ideas very clearly

- G B Leatherwood: It has been moved by Sergio that we adopt Adriano's presentation. Do I hear a second?

- Kim Peart: Scott - a vision of liberty is a philosophy that leads to action

- Kim Peart: Second

- Stephanie Lynne Thorburn: That action must be achievable- and first involves support, hence the need for strategy and philosophy on communication, prior to the action being possible. Yes, Adriano's 'final resolution' is a well constructed document.

- G B Leatherwood: It has been moved by Sergio and seconded by Kim that we adopt Adriano's presentation. Any further discussion?

- Scott Brown: Liberty is freedom from instituions and governments, etc.

- Camilo Andres Reyes: ;)

- Sergio Lebid: True Scott, what is the address to that place? (angel)

- Adriano Autino: R. A. Heinlein: governments are painful like bowles movements, but we cannot live without bowles movements (more or less)

- Keith Henson: that sounds like a strange translation/retranslation of Heinlein

- Kim Peart: The Italian translation

- Adriano Autino: @Keith sorry, i don't remember exactly, and have no time to look for the exact sentence, the meaning was that however

- Adriano Autino: ok, mr. chairman, i think we should vote?

- Camilo Andres Reyes: let's vote

- Kim Peart: Clean up our act with a vote

- Scott Brown: I want liberty from NSS, NASA, NSF, and all the rest that have failed us.

- Angelle: In response to Adriano suggestion, Aye

- Camilo Andres Reyes: failed us?? what do u mean?

- G B Leatherwood: Do I hear a call for the vote? If so, one point about our voting on this: Since we do not have an easily accessible membership roster, we will allow anyone here to vote. All in favor of adopting Adriano's presentation, signify by saying (writing) "Aye," opposed, "No."

- Sergio Lebid: Aye

- Camilo Andres Reyes: AYE

- Adriano Autino: @Scott, we make a serious criticism of those agencies, in our Issue I approved by this congress

- Jennifer Bolton: aye

- Jesús Raygoza: AYE.

- perez.saul: aye

- Kim Peart: Scott - "and he grinned that grin of defiance upon which, all freedom, ultimately rests" James Michener

- Kim Peart: Yes

- Scott Brown: Yes

- C.A. Chicoine: Aye

- Adriano Autino: "Government! Three- fourths parasitic and the rest stupid fumbling - oh, Harshaw concluded that man, a social animal, could not avoid government, any more than an individual could escape bondage to his bowels. But simply because an evil was inescapable was no reason to term it "good." He wished that government would wander off and get lost! (96)"

— Robert A. Heinlein (Stranger in a Strange Land)

- Stephanie Lynne Thorburn: Yes. And I think the feedback from the Congress should be useful in making the document more easy to operationalise as policy.

- G B Leatherwood: Any more votes- - without commentary, that is?

- Stephanie Lynne Thorburn: I was just clarifying if any ammendments were to be made..

- Camilo Andres Reyes: ;) it's ok

- G B Leatherwood: No, none. Just comments.

- Camilo Andres Reyes: ok, let's continue

- G B Leatherwood: Seeing no further votes, and seeing no "No" votes, I declare the motion passed.

[18.18.11] Congress Day 4 – Discussion and vote the Financial Balance

The Financial Balance was presented and approved.

[19.09.48] Congress Day 4 – Discussion and vote on the Executive Committee

- Adriano Autino:

ok, I will try to stay in 20 minutes, with my report

so we can close our works in time

as a summary i would say that

The First SRI Congress created the fundamentals to begin building the international organization:

- a true Executive Committee, composed by members who discussed and agreed a shared methodology

- a Public Relations Committee, including persons which hold skills and experience in journalism and media interfacing

- three projects, one of which already owns a working committee

What we really need is to have a simple structure, with few organs, each one of them can work autonomously, and coordineate themselves at organization level.

and have a simple hierarchical structure, so we can distribute the works and check the progress

seems simple, but of course it is not... :)

Our task today will be:

- to approve the executive committee and its work methodology
- to solicit a volunteer chairperson for each committee
- to take responsibility, each SRI member, to develop our projects and campaigns, first of all the members registration campaign

I will also briefly inform about teh status of the three projects, that is already more advanced than one could expect

2.1.1. Virtual Orbital Space Settlement

The VOSS is the most advanced project, just two weeks after its announcement.

We have:

a) a google group

b) a Second Life group, alive and working

c) an high level requirements document, prepared by K. Peart

d) a draft Statement of Work, prepared by A. Autino

The project immediate needs are the following ones:

- to confirm the chairperson of the project
- to choose a project manager
- to define the project development processes (included as TBD in the SOW)
- to define a project plan and basic funding needs (included as TBD in the SOW)

The chairperson should define the High Level Requirements (HLR) of the project, namely:

- the global vision and the main goals of the project
- the expectations of the different stakeholders and our intended benefits to them (civilization, academic world, students, SRI, other communities, institutions, space and non space)

- the foreseen main milestones and deadlines

the above role is covered by Kim, that I will nominate as chair of the project

Kim is also the originator of the idea

The project manager should be encharged to move from the above HLR, complete the SOW, define the project WorkBreakdown Structure and Work packages description, organize the working team, assigning roles, defining deadlines, development methodologies, verification plans, detailed milestones.

both the chair and the pm shall work in synergy, since this is a complex and very ambitious project, and includes both artistic issues and management ones

so the VOSS project is the most advanced one, currently

the other two projects, the Civilization Risk Assessment & management and the Best Space Industrial Development line are at the starting blocks

they both need:

volunteers, a chairperson and a project manager.

   Works to be developed:

- High Level Requirements document
- Statement of Work
- Project development and verification plan

as it was to be expected, many people gave their availability for the Virtual project, and very few for the other two

this project should trade- off the most promising space development industrial lines, and indicate which ones have the numbers for contributing to open the space frontier

however, each project committee will be free to design their chirpersons and project managers, and the Executive Committee will of course indicate some preferences

the congress doesn't need to vote the projects committees

since we already voted the projects, at the end of day 2

ok, this point is over, for me

i just want to underline that all of our committees are working teams

and not just consultive teams or discussion clubs
it means that:
if a committee is inactive for more than 3 months it will be recycled
the chair will loose the chair
the members are expected to be pro- active and propose volunteer activities
not to expect tasks coming from someone else
my worst feeling is when a committee was expected to do something and it keep silent...
then i don't knwo if i have to ring the wake, or what to do...
so please accept to be in a committee only if you plan to think, to be autonomous, propositive and collaborative
if you don't feel like that, please don't accept the role
The SRI Executive Committee, just after the Congress, will start developing the following plan:

    a)   2011 membership registration campaign
    b)   Kick- off the three SRI main projects, as decided by this congress
    c)   Check the work in progress and supervise the four main committees: PR, VOSS, BSID, CRAM
    d)   Draw a Funding Plan, listing potential donors and foundations to be contacted
    e)   Draw a Business Plan for the SRI as a non profit association, how to develop our proposal at international level, defining proper goals and measurement milestones
    f)   Draw a plan for outreach, including: conferences, subjects for communications and press releases, commenting the relevant actuality events

- Keith Henson: I wish someone could point me to a study of space tourism that shows it can make money

- G B Leatherwood: Keith, that is what Project 2 is to do- - look at the possible space industrual development avenues and prioritize them for our support.

- Adriano Autino: @Keith, in our book "Three Theses for the Space Renaissance" you will find what you are looking for: the second chapter is all on that subject (Space Tourism and SBSP)

- G B Leatherwood: We have reached the end of our planned meeting, but not the end of our agenda. We have a choice: Continue the meeting until you have given us the membership of the Exec. Comm. or deliver it via e- mail to all our members.

- Adriano Autino:

The proposed members of the SRI Executive Committee:

- A. V. Autino (SRI President)
- Gail B. Leatherwood (Secretaire General)
- Feng Hsu
- Kim Peart
- Maria Catalina
- Scott Von Brown
- Neda Ansari
- Sean Con
- Walt Putnam
- Jesus Raygoza

Besides the above persons, the members of the SRI Board and SRI Founders (Patrick Collins, Alberto Cavallo, Sergio Lebid, Julio Gonzales- Saenz) have a permanent right to sit in the Executive Committee, and:

- be noticed of all meetings of the Executive
- take part to said meetings
- and exercise their vote.

The Executive will have faculty to invite other SRI members to its meetings, in order to support the coordination of the SRI works, with special attention to coordinators and/or supporters of local chapters.

The above list and criteria were approved by the congress.

Chapter III

The Final Resolution

Summarizing the achievements of the SRI First Congress

Approaching the conclusion of our first international congress, we can say that our tenacity and patience, to hold this congress, though just online, was prized, in terms of participation and high quality of the discussion we had.

Such a high level of discussion allowed us to get several relevant achievements, in theory and in practice, with some new organizational structures, which began to work in these two weeks, even before the congress was completed!

In summary, we were able to identify some key items, to be addressed in our outreach communication effort:

- <u>fighting the abysmal lack of knowledge and continuing misinformation</u> around the most promising space industrial developments, such as Space Tourism and SBSP
- <u>bringing some rather neglected space topics to the public attention</u>, such as space debris, human life and health protection against hard radiation in space and low/zero gravity, astrobiology in general, exo-agricolture and exo-farming, Near Earth Asteroids capture and mining, all topics very relevant for a serious space settlement plan
- <u>enhancing the public awareness about the global civilization risk</u>, paying special attention to the communication methods, and always associating this argument with our message of hope, pointing out that this is a growth crisis for our civilization, while the birth of a Civilization spanning the Solar System is approaching
- <u>bringing a wind of innovation in the political / ideological environment</u>, with our proposal to replace the obsolete ideologies of liberalism and socialism by astronautic humanism, based on compassion, exo-development, assuring abundance of resources for free and democratic civil development

- running a visionary project, the Virtual Orbital Space Settlement, that will be able to catch the imagination and raise hope in the future into the true heritage of humanity: the children of the Earth
- running two other projects, the Civilization Risk Assessment & Management and spotting the Best Space Business Industrial Development, to engage researchers, universities and students in the urgent needs of our civilization, to step over the current global crisis and finally aiming high again

The congress also allowed us to make some essential organizational improvements, giving birth to two very important committees:

- the SRI Executive Committee, that for the first time in our still brief history, can become the true direction for our international association
- the SRI Public Relations Committee, that is already drawing its Plan, and in these days sent our first Press Release to a relevant number of media and agencies

The large interest arrised from our congress inspired many new supporters to join us, especially from the South East regions, such as India, Nepal, Malaysia, and others. The founding nucleus of the SRI India Chapter has been born, and now we will have to provide proper coordination for this very exciting effort that can be reproduced in many other countries, where we have supporters and sympathizers, if not yet registered members.

After this congress, the SRI is stronger then before, and this is not to be measured only by membership and active support, but also in our increased capacity to agree on methodologies and to take initiatives in a team spirit.

And maybe it is not a case that we are celebrating our first congress while the Shuttle Atlantis is flying for the last time. As many newspapers are writing, this the end of an age: the age of space used for Earth.

And a new age is beginning: the age of the space used for human development outside Earth, or exo-development.

The age of Space Renaissance

Political guidelines emerging from the congress, for our public outreach viral campaign

Few words to explain the meaning of the term '*exo-development*'. E could use '*space development*', and maybe within our community it would be clear enough, but I think exo-development is more appropriate: when people will ask what we mean, we will have a chance to develop our discourse.

'Exo-development' means human industrial development out of Earth, while the term 'space development' was used traditionally for any space business, including the telecommunication satellites during the 40 years of use of space for Earth. Exo-development means use space for human development outside Earth, the new strategy, as Jeff Greason indicated clearly. According to David Dunlop, NSS is talking about bootstrapping the exo-development too.

Fighting Misinformation, toward Exo-Development

The privatization of space - key to open the high frontier

We keep on reading and observing in the media, superficial and misleading opinions about space tourism. According to these views, space tourism would be a kind of very expensive amusement for rich people. Some of these opinions charge space tourism with immorality in a time of crisis, as a waste of money and valuable resources.

Since we don't only talk inside the space community, we shall develop a *wide popular campaign*, against such positions, focusing on commonsense with public opinion, the key elements of which are the following.

Space tourism – pioneered by Patrick Collins and David Ashford since the early 90's – got a boost by Gregg Maryniak and Peter Diamandis in 1996[1], when they gave birth to the X-Prize, granting $10 million to the first private company able to fly at 100 km, carrying three passengers and repeating the flight within a couple of weeks, after refuelling and maintenance of the vehicle.

---

[1] This paragraph was changed (July 12th 2011) after the vote of the Congress (July 9th 2011), accepting a remark given by Jan MacKinlay, with his letter to the SRI President. The previous formulation was historically uncorrect.

From a field of 20 entrants, Burt Rutan's Scaled Composites won the prize in 2004, with the legendary suborbital craft Space Ship One, with a project costing less than US $30 million.

This ground-breaking event triggered a number of processes that were not yet fully realised. First was the crisis with the large space agencies, charged for their absurdly high costs: each flight of the Space Shuttle has cost $500 million, about 17 times the cost of SpaceShipOne.

Space Ship One demonstrated that the cost to orbit can be downsized and that the *privatization of space* is no longer in the realm of science fiction, but can be a reality.

When we wrote our book "Three Theses for the Space Renaissance", the number of companies in the new space industry has grown by magnitude, from 20 companies in 2004 to more than 100 and some of them (Virgin galactic) are well positioned to develop the suborbital tourism industry. Others, such as Bigelow and SpaceX, aim directly for the Earth Orbit market, developing inflatable hotel accommodation and low cost orbital vehicles.

Space Tourism, starting at suborbital and progressing to orbital, is the business segment that can progressively grow, accumulating capital for progressively improving the technologies, until a fully Reusable Launch Vehicle is achieved.

Therefore, despite its unhappy name of 'tourism' (something to be made just for fun), space tourism, or *civilian space passengers transportation*, or *civilian space flight*, has an incomparably high social value, as the sole business development that could, by its force alone, open the space frontier.

If civilian space flight will lead to synergies with other promising developments, including SBSP and will, supported by government grants and fiscal discounts, make the difference and achieve what humanity desperately needs before 2020: a true full RLV.

Therefore our line is to solicit both government support and increased private investments in this industry, the only one that will assure a return when the space economy will really take off.

This story shall be communicated and repeated everywhere, since it is continuously the target of both interested and ideological attacks and criticisms.

The SRI holds several champions of this story (Patrick Collins, first of all), and our PR Committee should interview them with regularity, to always gain fresh information on the latest developments and achievements.

This will not be our only song, however we should keep on singing it (☺).

Space Based Solar Power - key to the Space Development

If Space Tourism is the preferred ideological target of backward-thinking *anti-capitalist* ideologists, SBSP is the preferred target of vested interests in oil and other well-entrenched energy lobbies.

Energy beams from space have been the subject of endless conspiracy theories and withering scrutiny, despite a 2009 NASA study that concluded microwaves from space would be slightly less intense than the Sun's rays and would pose no danger to people.

We also discussed, in our congress, about the risk that SBSP could represent another Earth-only-targeted business for next 40 years, which became the case with telecommunication satellites, scuttling astronautics in this field after Apollo 11. Dr Feng Hsu, a member of the SRI Board since its beginning, argued that SBSP could never be realized without a true RLV technology.

Dr Hsu position is quite reasonable, if we think that the cost of Earth-based solar energy is still too high to be competitive with the other energy sources. The earthly photovoltaic industry stays on the market only because of government incentives: when the money runs out, such industries fail and many people are jobless again.

Let's think what it would be like to fly power satellites with the expendable rocket technology: SBSP could never hope to be competitive!

SBSP, in order to take off, desperately needs RLV and low cost to orbit technologies. Therefore SBSP is not exactly a learning industry, like civilian space flight. We shall promote synergies between the SBSP research and the validation of technologies for low cost access to orbit. Also see this paper "Synergies Between Solar Power Supply from Space and Passenger Space Travel" by our Patrick Collins on the SpaceFuture web site.

We also need to consider how to promote SBSP, where there is an immense quantity of technical and engineering work to be done. People tend to undervalue the effort required. Consider that nothing has been sent into orbit, so far, in the field of energy and nobody funds anything that is not already demonstrated as a working option...

Considering the very huge effort still to be made to fly demonstrators and then building the first operative plants, this is still mainly a matter for governments and international cooperation: after throwing so much public money out the window (absurd military expense, just for an example), this would be a very worthwhile use of public funding.

Having achieved the low cost access to orbit, establishing space based solar plants is the logical next step, in the direction of exo-industry development.

We should make it definitely clear, that the space solar plants are indispensable to all space development in the Geo-Lunar space region. The SBSP stations will fuel hotels, industrial orbiting platforms, and ion-propulsion passenger and cargo vehicles for any destination.

Without SBSP, no exo-development program can happen.

If directed to Earth rectennas, the SBSP energy will also contribute to solve the energy problems on Earth, though this may not be their main goal.

This vision, strongly projected outward and upward, shall be communicated everywhere, always countering any Earth-centric view that would confine SBSP to Earth use alone.

Raising public attention on some disciplines essential for Space Development

As Jeff Greason said in his address to ISDC 2011, space settlement was never the strategy for any space agency so far. Therefore some research lines were neglected.

Space debris

With almost 6000 tonnes of trash in the space above Earth orbit, a life-threatening danger now confronts all astronautics, especially when we will really start flying, working and living in the space beyond Earth.

From another point of view, orbital debris also represent 6000 tonnes of materials that are already outside the Earth gravitational well. As this material has already cost a lot of money (20K / Kg, more or less $120 billions). Most of this investment will be burned in the atmosphere as the orbits of each item decays. Should we collect the biggest items at least, to help build the space infrastructure?

It is also interesting to note that a technology to move quickly and easily among different orbits still doesn't exist. The development of this kind of technology continues to be a prime interest for the military (moving fast among orbits, to catch possible hostile satellites), but it could be of interest to civilian astronautics too, with a view to a large debris recovery program.

In our vision for bootstrapping exo-development, cleaning debris from orbit is a critical step: especially as any increase human spaceflight will inevitably raise the probability of impacts with debris, where even a small item with a high velocity presents a risk.

Human life and health protection against space hard radiations and low/zero gravity

These are topics of enormous importance for any serious civilian space flight development program.

Protection against radiation is essentially a matter of shielding. Therefore the studies related to shields shall be boosted, even vs. the many science fiction items with which our scientists like to play taxpayer support (an aggressive position will not be discounted in our outreach). Inflatable shields seem very promising in this regard and the use of water as well, when a Moon water extraction industry will be available.

Astrobiology research in general shall be boosted too, like exo-agricolture and exo-farming, all topics very relevant for a serious space settlement plan.

As far as the low and zero gravity threat to human health and physiology is concerned, the most immediate answer is to build big spinning habitats, like we will develop in our Virtual Orbiting Space Settlement project. Other possibilities are a traded-off, such as medical countermeasures.

Near Earth Asteroids capture and mining

The general understanding of this matter is that NEA mining will be feasible in a near future, as the effort needed to "jump" on some NEA's is not that critical.

The orbits of some of these objects pass quite near Earth – which also present a danger, of course – on more or less the same eclyptic plan, therefore the delta-V needed to reach them is surprisingly low. Of course, since we want to extract minerals from them, we will have to follow the objects in their orbit around the Sun (they could even pass dangerously near it!) or to schedule short missions, catching them when they fly nearest to Earth in their orbit.

However, the age of exploiting exo-resources could begin earlier than people may now imagine.

Heralding a new breeze of innovation in the political / ideological environment

As we wrote in our Issue I for this congress, we keep on voting for collectivist or liberist utopias, but we are expected to be satisfied by real socialism and real liberalism, both of which have famously failed, as demonstrated by a long series of terrible catastrophes. The current political leaderships of our globalized society are demonstrably inadequate to the challenges now being faced.

It is time to replace those obsolete ideologies – that have repeatedly demonstrated their tragic inadequacy – with a brand new ideology: astronautic humanism, based on compassion for all humans and for all the sentient beings.

Astronautic humanism is the sole philosophy that can claim to support seven billion people in their aims to fully realize their happiness, and to give expression to a fully inclusive civilization, having the material, cultural and spiritual means to apply a true compassion, honour and dignity toward all. Our resources and energy are based on space development, assuring the boundless abundance of resources of the Solar System, to develop a Solar Civilization of thousand trillions human beings, a wide free market of thousands trillions, a multicultural society based on millions of communities, each one developing their preferred values and cultural diversification, able to exchange their experiences and achievements, toward a true human status, though bodies shapes and physiologies will of course progressively differ.

Counting on the trillions comets made of ice and basic life components, and orbiting around our Solar System in the immense Oort Cloud, our offspring will never die of starvation or thirst.

The power of astronautic humanism is that it will never seek to impose any "ideal social model" to anybody, since the immense resources of the Solar System, the Kuiper Belt and the Oort Cloud, will allow an endless democratic revolution, and the conditions of scarcity of resources that favour the growth of bureaucratic powers will never rise again in human history.

The history of the past demonstrates that, more than the social model, the moral qualities of the leaders are highly relevant in human communities and national governance.

Astronautic Humanism is the sole ideology that will allow each community the complete freedom of experimenting the preferred social models.

Orbiting cities and islands in space will favour self-government and direct democracy, much more than large nations. It could be in space communities that humans will find again, in another environmental dimension, the human sized relationships, where each one is appreciated and respected for their abilities.

Astronautic Humanism is the sole ideology that can support the birth of a social environment in which each one can *aim and get what their imagination can conceive* and where the people with less imagination will not need to be angry and jealous, since the general abundance of resources will allow everybody to share everything. That kind of society is likely the nearest thing to a society where people will have the realization of their own happiness.

We are aware this is a utopian view, but it is the highest utopia ever conceived and by means of astronautic humanism every utopia becomes feasible, so why not the highest one possible?

Is this the end or the beginning of the space age?

On June 30th The Economist published an article titled *"The end of the Space Age: Inner space is useful. Outer space is history"*.[13]

The article postulates simply that, with the last flight of space shuttle Atlantis, the space age has ended. "Space tourism" says the article "is a luxury service that is, in any case, unlikely to go beyond low-Earth orbit at best (the cost of getting even as far as the moon would reduce the number of potential clients to a handful). The other source of revenue is ferrying astronauts to the benighted International Space Station (ISS), surely the biggest waste of money, at $100 billion and counting, that has ever been built in the name of science."

The article contemptuously calls us (space advocats) "space cadets", and teases us saying that Obama is talking about our "ultimate dream", a mission to Mars in 2030.

I think this article is the best sample of what the real society and economists in particular, think about the new space industry – a market that "seems small and vulnerable". In this aspect, at least, they sadly confirm our analysis: the new space industry likely will not make it through the current economic crises, without a vigorous public support. The position expressed in the Economist fails to consider the emerging space economy as an alternative to the crisis!

The article also says that space -- the inner space, inside Earth Orbit – worked greatly for Earth business during the last 40 years: exactly as we say in our analysis: the satellite age was excellent for earthly business, but not for astronautics and not for the advancement of human civilization!

In this article we can see clearly the place from where we must start and how long the road ahead will be. Our problem is one of time, as the need for action is now critical.

How to answer to lobbyists and ideological adversaries

One of our main tasks is: *how to answer the Economist.*

Will our answer be effective enough, should we try to reply on a purely terrestrial business level?

Of course not! If we want to be effective, and catch the people's attention, showing the cultural ignorance of the economist's approach to global problems, we have to use our analysis of the Civilization global risk.

It was said, in our discussion: "despite the end of world forecasts of the catastrophists, the world is always spinning around in the cosmos".

It was also proposed that we should point out more of the positive aspects of our proposals, in order not to scare people.

However, we shall consider (see the book "Three Theses for the Space Renaissance", chapter "The Status of Civilization") that we are living in unprecedented times, characterized by the global extension of several social and physical processes:

- the world never had seven billions inhabitants before
- the world was never 70% industrialized
- the world never had before repeated default of countries, such as Argentina, Ireland, Greece, Portugal, ...
- the world has never before had a rate of "apocalypse size" disasters so high, e.g. tsunamis, earthquakes, hurricanes, oil spills (Gulf of Mexico 2010), nuclear accidents following earthquake and tsunamis (Japan 2011)
- the world has never before had a global economic crises like the current one, which started in 2008 and has yet to end.

Other growing concerns at this time include:

- a global shortage of fish and other food resources (also due to use of agriculture for energy generation)
- a shortage of fresh water
- global pollution and decay of the human living environment
- acidification of the oceans, due to excess of CO_2 (also due to increasing use of coal by China for energy production)

Only the Space Renaissance has an explanation for the above. We call it *the closed world syndrome*. We are facing the incredible contradiction between a growing population, meaning potentially larger markets and at the same time a decrease of jobs!

Such contradiction can be caused only by a general shortage of resources and energy!

Yes, when the world reached similar conditions -- though they were never global like nowaday!—it always kept on spinning; but how? By terrible wars and blood baths.

The risk of a global civilization (unrecoverable) crash is very real. This is nothing to be scared of, but a challenge that we can take on and fight against.

Astronautic humanists are dead against wars as a way to 'solve' the problems of the Earth and we have the good alternative: exo-development, in the outer space!

Nobody else promotes this analysis – except Stephen Hawking and a few others, mostly unheeded – and nobody else is proposing a global solution. We do, and shall keep on doing it, amplifying our voice many times.

The extreme ecologist position

Ideological adversaries, such as radical ecologists (mainly in Europe), will put forward their Earth-limited thought, as if the only ecology to take care of was the Earth's surface! They even don't care about space debris, since they don't see it (they never raise their eyes to the sky…).

Their answer to the global metaphysical warming is to hide their head in the sand, to de-industrialize the world and decrease the economy (they call themselves supporters of the "happy decrease") and pray to the nature goddess to save their lives…

These are backward positions that shall be faced and opposed, mainly by the European SRI members.

There is a huge struggle to be undertaken, in favour of quality, culture and good technologies against decrepit ideological positions that bring these movements to say NO, by default, to any technological project: first they say NO, then they look for reasons to support their position.

There's another (more rare) category of ecologists, with those who include the solar system in their reflection, but just to say that we, humans, don't have the right to change the environments of the Moon or Mars and that we should leave them untouched.

Of course, we will discuss such a position, since nobody lives on the Moon or Mars, except maybe some viruses and/or simple vegetable form of life.

We can argue that comets and asteroids are quite volatile components of the Solar System, including the Oort Cloud System. The comets are subject to losing most of their mass, when they come near the

Sun. Having asteroids with very unsteady orbits that are often captured by Jupiter and hurled into the inner solar system.

Therefore, using such materials for life support and building orbital cities and islands in space, which environment would we change? Nothing that wasn't already destined to change very quickly, and in many cases to vaporise without being used by anyone!

The "common sense" positions

Many people say:
- going to space? first we should solve problems on Earth,
- now we are not mature, but maybe in one century…,
- now we don't have money, maybe in 20 years, when the economy has recovered…
- the tendency of people toward inertia, that the world is always spinning, despite all of the cassandras, etc...

The rationale listed in previous paragraphs applies. Besides,
- the birth rate is decreasing, and trends say the demographic vector will revert before 2050: this is the true danger, an older and older society, on the way into the sunset...
- if we remain on Earth, human history is in its old age
- if we expand into space, our species is very young, and our civilization will be at the dawn of a new era, counted in millennia, not centuries
- the point is that exo-development shall be bootstrapped now, or our civilization is condemned, as not just us, but a living genius like Stephen Hawking said

Our mission is based on the above global risk, concerning events that will occur within this century.

Otherwise the need would not be that urgent.

Shouldn't we be able to communicate such urgency?

If we are silent, we will have failed our mission.

The birth of a Baby Solar Civilization

How is the best way to communicate our analysis and proposals?

This will be a task for our PR Committee, and for our creative intelligence.

The only effective answer to the Economist's and other foolish positions, by increasing public awareness of the extreme danger humanity is going to face.

Who will we believe? Stephen Hawking or the lobbies who led the civilization into the current cul de sac?

This is a critical point:

The Space Renaissance would lose its scope and mission, should it change its nature from a philosophical association, to entertain radical positions to reduce human numbers on Earth, or promote forms of collective suicide: there are already too many views of this kind at large.

We also have a positive metaphor, which we can keep using: when we wrote "Earth is not sick: She's Pregnant!" it was a great self-explaining metaphor.

It means that this is a growth crisis, for our civilization, since we have the technological and cultural means to expand to a larger ecological niche.

Should we not having such means, than our world will be a tunnel, with no way out for our civilization, if not our species.

Should we deny the right of the Earth to give birth, it would be a way for killing both Mother Nature and her baby Solar Civilization!

We shall say the truth about the labour pains, and about the extremely critical period of the birth, including the tremendous risk of stillbirth. We will also present the possibility of a happy event, of we will be accurate, firm and long-sighted in our vision.

With our communication we shall always present the two alternatives:

- the death by stillbirth of our civilization, should the world remain closed
- an unprecedented age of social and economic growth, with the birth of the Solar Civilization and the Space Renaissance.

The three projects, to balance our communication

Our three projects present the right answer to all of our communications needs during the next four years:

The Civilization Risk Assessment & Management project will deepen the global civilization risk and the countermeasures (provide enough *midwives* to help Gaia in her childbirth). We will use this project to communicate with all the scientific and non scientific communities potentially interested to analyzing the future of our civilization and related challenges.

The Best Space Industrial Development project will trade-off the different space business lines, in order to fight the Economist-like positions by solid figures, not only through our very reasonable social analysis. We will use this project to communicate with all the economic and sociological communities potentially interested in analyzing the future of the globalized economy and the related challenges.

The Virtual Orbital Space Settlement project will develop a realistic model environment. We will use it to communicate with all the young and less young people who would like to experience what life could be like in an orbital space settlement, city or island. This project will offer the joy of playing, a human natural behaviour, that stimulates creativity indeed, as well as opportunities for scientific enquiry into how human communities in space could function.

Chapter IV — 2012 - The Final Resolution Upgrade

One year after the first SRI congress, the global crisis is worse, and SRI's task is clearer.

Resolution approved by the SRI Executive Committee during the July 14-15th 2012 Meeting

Author: Adriano V. Autino, Editing and contributes: Julio Gonzales-Saenz, Gail B. Leatherwood, Patrick Q. Collins, Alberto Cavallo, Jesus Raygoza, Susan Singer, Kim Peart, Sergio Lebid

Civilization status – an upgrade

Our analysis keeps entirely its validity

In our ISSUE I document – "our philosophical understanding of the status of civilization and the SRI political program 2011 – 2015", we summarized the status of the civilization, as follows (The Metaphysics of Astronautics).

From 1950 to 1970 humanity made its first steps in orbit, flying some tens of pioneers, and reaching the Moon in 1969 with the historic enterprise of Collins, Armstrong and Aldrin. Twenty percent of the world was industrialized, human population was 3.7 billion. The space ocean was still clean and pristine, nothing but meteorites crossed the interface between Earth and the cosmos.

From 1970 to 2000, Earth's orbit was filled by iron boxes for telecommunication and earth observation. The moon was forgotten, and industrialization kept on growing up only on the surface of our mother planet. Earth human population in year 2000 reached 6 billion. The space ocean near Earth was filled with garbage. The strategy and focus of human space activities was Earth & Business. The estimated total mass of space debris was about 5,500 tons. Current (2012) estimation of orbiting debris (NASA): More than 21,000 orbital debris larger than

10 cm, approximately 500,000 particles between 1 and 10 cm in diameter, more than 100 million particles smaller than 1 cm^4. From 2000 to nowadays Earth's orbit kept on being filled by thousands of satellites for TV, Earth observation, and scientific payloads. Nothing was done to claim the orbit and clean/reuse the garbage, i.e. begin to inhabit the orbit. The main space agencies are in deep crisis. India, China and Brazil have begun their industrialization, and rapidly aim to the first places as economic powers. Earth human population passed 7 billion. Fertility is sadly declining in all the world areas, and Earth is closed in a cage of iron garbage. The strategy and focus of the human space activities is caged by the interest of greedy lobbies: oil, weapons, and bankers. Civilization is in the middle of a process we could call *"Metaphysical warming"*, a mix of: true or perceived lack of resources and energy, people's rights demand, environmental decay, resource wars, growing population, global industrialization, fear of the future, waiting for a huge holocaust, or Armageddon.

The growing complexity in a closed environment leads to an unsustainable increase of pressure, as testified by all social, economic, environmental, and political indicators. The signs of what Stephen Hawking called "implosion of the civilization" are already visible, on a path of failures and disasters, both natural and those caused by the human risk assessment immaturity. The Chernobyl disaster represented the ideological bankruptcy of the Stalinist Soviet regime and its ideology. A low-quality ideology produces low-quality science. If this was and still remains true for the old-fashioned Soviet nuclear power plants, kept working in defiance of every principle of security of the population, it is certainly true for the Gulf of Mexico in 2010 and for Fukushima in 2011. Such two disasters represent the failure of liberal ideology. A key problem of the advanced world economy today is the lack of new industries which are needed to replace the old industries shipped out to China, India and elsewhere. The popular demand for new industries will grow to large scale. The new economic powers, China, India, and Brazil, are experiencing a season of growth, and the people there are aimed by a strong hope of development and progress to achieve the same wealth level of the postindustrial countries. But such aims already knew a serious standstill with the global crisis beginning in 2008 and not yet terminated. It appears obvious to anyone willing to see the reality, that the resources, energy sources and environmental capabilities of Earth are not enough to sustain the civil development of a civilization of seven billion people, and the limit will be reached even earlier, given the limits of today's political systems.

One year after writing the above concepts, nobody can anymore deny them, the situation has worsened, and governments are desperately seeking means to avoid a global economic bankruptcy. Maybe the European Union will find enough courage to become a Federal Union, like the United States (nobody ever even suggested to kick Louisiana or other poor states out of the USA, so why Greece, Spain or Ireland and others should be kicked out of the USE?). Or maybe not. The fundamentals of the global crisis will not change. The crisis was triggered by fraudulent US financial products, but is reaching its deeper effect in Europe, where the strategy was more oriented to degrowth and have a so-called "soft landing". Now the political leaders have discovered that growth is a necessity, and are frantically looking for a growth policy. But all they are able to think of is to target some money for infrastructure and public works. That might help, of course, but, considering the depth of this crisis, could it be enough?

Definitely not. The claimed growth strategies are that poor because they are still supported by a degrowth, closed world, philosophy.

This **global crisis** is more and more revealing itself as *the crisis of the closed world philosophy*, whatever the immediate catalyst this time, and the only solution can come from bootstrap the space economy, based on a development of civilian astronautics. The crisis has already lasted, worsening, for four years, and many commentators say it will last 10 years, at least. Nicolai Kondratiev[5], a Russian economist who died in a Stalinist gulag, analyzed the history of economy since 1800 and found a cycle of 60 years. Each crisis lasts 20 years, more or less. But the current crisis, considering its global character and deep combined causes and effects —impending shortage of resources, lack of jobs, immature competition for resources and energy, environmental decay —could be the last one, and directly lead to civilization's implosion.

All of the symptoms we analyzed one year ago have worsened, reinforcing our analysis.

The SRI task we identified – to accelerate the space renaissance through the rapid development of the civilian astronautic industry and economy – is becoming more and more urgent, and it could be easier, in the current environment of a long lasting and worsening crisis, to explain our alternative to the general public. In fact, the main concern of the general public, about *where their next meal will come from*, is more and more in line with the concern *for the survival of civilization*.

A necessary actualization about energy and raw materials

Shale gas, methane and natural gas in general are likely a real alternative to oil. Should we look at current reality only from the quantitative point of view, we could conclude that the world is *not* running out of energy, at least in the short term. Americans' electricity bills are falling (and America's CO2 output is even falling) as electricity companies switch from dirty coal to clean gas (essentially methane - which isn't even poisonous). America is about to become a net energy exporter. Britain, Germany, Poland have all found huge shale gas deposits which promise to reduce Europe's dependence on Russian energy supplies . On top of this, conventional gas supplies continue to increase: a Japanese-American consortium has just found the largest ever gas-field off Mozambique.

First consideration, SBSP is not an immediate necessity, to feed Earthling further development, provided that this would be a worth task. It is also to be remarked, however, that *methane is a real greenhouse gas*, ten times more than CO2, though CO2 was indicated as the worst *greenhouse devil*, during the last decades. One of the possible causes of the big saurians extinction (alternative to the famous meteorite), is a giant green-house effect, caused by the huge methane output by these big animals, basically eating woody branches.

On another layer of the discourse, if the price of energy will decrease, this could be a breath for the world economy. But, does this new abundance of Earth energy sources mitigate or delay the general risk of civilization implosion? If yes, what could be the amount of time achieved? What is the environmental cost of extraction of the shale gas? The impact could be even worse than extracting oil muds, since the shale gas extraction requires to crush the rock. And, most importantly of all, does this concept (*"we are NOT (yet) running our of energy"*) change the sign of our strategic address? (*"mother planet is not enough for seven billion people"*).

In our congress discussion, we wrote that civilization entered a thread of "metaphysical warming", in which the pressure in a closed environment is growing higher and higher. Such analysis remains correct, and the discover of new Earthling energy sources doesn't decrease the pressure, but contribute to raise it however.

The matter is not where we take energy, on Earth or in space. The true point is how and where we will use the energy:

a) to further develop Earth industry **OR**
b) to develop exo-planetary infrastructure and industry.

Scenario a) will further increase the pressure, worsening the risk of civilization implosion. While the scenario b) will reduce the pressure on Earth, **and** disclose an incalculable economic and cultural development.

Of course the civilian astronautic industry shall be developed on Earth, for several decades to come at least, therefore we need a) however. We shouldn't be scared at all about a further pressure increase, if it is targeted to open the system. **What we should strongly oppose is a pressure increase driven by immature leaders, once again convinced that everything can go on on this planet like it went during the last two centuries, and we can afford lying on the bottom of the Earth's gravitational well, avoiding any expansion outside.** Therefore we should plause the new energy source, since it could provide a breath from the global crisis, and allow to develop the civilian astronautic industry.

But we shall be even more determined, indicating the absolute imperative of the expansion beyond the Earth boundaries.

As to the food resources and metal raw materials, our analysis should not change: if we (seven billion) are not running out right now we (7,5 - 8 billion) will, in few years. The markets already perceive it, and this is a strong factor of the current crisis. Always we should recall, when talking about humanity size, that the huge number and counting is by no means a disaster. For astronautic humanists 7 billion humans and more are the indispensable platform of intelligences needed to try the step to the stars.

The WorldFish Center and the International Food Policy Research Institute estimate that fish production would have to double in the

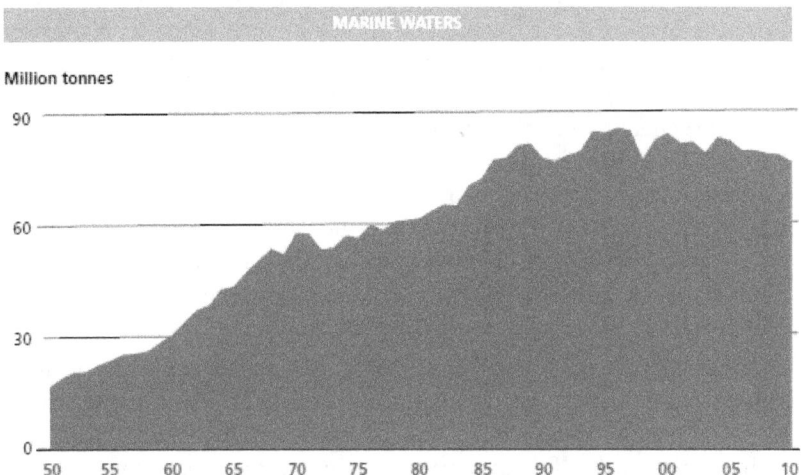

next 25 years to keep up with population growth. They say this is virtually impossible, and warn the shortfall could have disastrous consequences for more than a billion people in developing countries[6]. From the FAO report on fisheries and aquaculture, we learn that the global fishery in marine waters reached its maximum production in 1995, and is progressively declining.

"The State of World - Fisheries and Aquaculture 2012" FAO Fisheries and Aquaculture Department[7]. The aquaculture and sea-farming is growing, that's true.

In general, we can observe that, the longer the delay in moving our development to space, the more the wild life will disappear from planet Earth, not only on ground, but in the sea too. Whatever our personal feeling toward environmental issues and cares, we know that eliminating any wild sea area would be a quite critical milestone in human history on this planet, of which we are unable to calculate the consequences.

Human impact on biosphere and the risk of civilization implosion

What we should however observe is that the quantity of (Earthling) available energy resources is not the only variable, in the civilization implosion equation. A worsening of environmental conditions could be a catalyst of the definitive crisis, combined with the other agents we already analyzed several times. And methane is maybe more dangerous than oil, from the environmental point of view, being a true greenhouse gas. At this purpose Prof. Carlo Rubbia maybe 25 years ago proposed this concept: "there is not such thing like a clean and not polluting energy source". Any source, if applied at mass level, requires a price, in terms of pollution and environmental decay, including Earthling solar cells, that would cover huge ground superfices with black panels, making the ground unfertile. Neither SBSP to feed Earth would be an exception, since it would require hundreds of unmanned satellites again, further polluting orbits, and concentrating on Earth a huge amount of energy (increase of pressure).

What all analyzers never consider is that, for feeding seven billion people' basic needs and development needs, and the highest Maslov needs (since we are humanist, and consider all humans have equal right to happiness and self realization) whatever energy source should be exploited at mass level. And this planet, as observed by Hawking, Lovelock and many others, will not support it. That is the fundamental rationale for moving our development outside Earth atmosphere: release the pressure on Earth, give hope to the people, move our great number in a bigger ecologic niche.

This concept was already proposed by Dr. Marco C. Bernasconi in his 1997 paper "Why Implementing the Space Option Is Necessary for Society"[8]. From the abstract of that paper: *"On a planet soon to host a ten-billion population that will impact the biosphere's workings as never before, at a time when many governments and organizations see the virtue in the management of scarcity, musing on the origins of life and of the Solar System can hardly be expected to be invested with high priority. The Space Option arose from the analysis of the issues confronting humanity. In reviewing the material needs of the human population in the near future, the analysis finds that the impact on the biosphere will perforce be much larger than it usually seems to be acceptable to assume."*

So, the problem is not the availability of energy sources, but **our impact on the biosphere**. Considering the concept of biosphere and our impact on it, we are not just talking about nature, we are talking about the fusion of Earth nature and human culture, including everything: natural environment, economy, industry, technologies, development, crisis, arts, feelings, psicological mass tendencies, movements, fashions, energy, food, agriculture, jobs, hope, desperation, money, environment, raw sources, etc... The collapse of Biosphere can be initiated by any of the above listed variables and conditions, quickly involving other variables and conditions, in a kind of nuclear reaction.

Should the Earthling biosphere collapse, it would be a terrible catastrophe.

Should the Earthling biosphere collapse before civilization had assured its survival elsewhere, that would be an unrecoverable catastrophe: end of humankind.

Our bet is to ignite the space renaissance in time to avoid both such catastrophes. To do that we could choose to politically "ride" some of the popular bogeymen of these years, like the ones advertised by Mr. Al Gore.But our duty, as a philosophical association, is to be scientifically rigorous, and our agnosticism about the theory of the global warming remains the most correct position, since we never want to contribute to deceive the people.

Will the space revolution create million jobs? During this century, only a part of these jobs will be *phisically* in space. They will be mainly on Earth, if civilian astronautic will gain momentum. As already mentioned, a further Earthling industrial development will increase the pressure, and what we called "metaphysical warming" will worsen, for sure. But this is a risk we cannot avoid, if civilization wants to have a chance to go ahead. A risk, connected to a project, can be managed. The big risk of remaining confined to the ground, missing any project, would be thousand folds bigger and worse.

However, a kind of space race is under way

The current situation is characterized not only by bad conditions, that is, the worsening of the global crisis. Some quite positive events are also occurring.

In our theses we analyzed a new social subject: the influence of excellent entrepreneurs, born of the electronic revolution and mass information systems, with a sharp vision of the future, is growing more and more important. Some of the key themes we identified are taking place in the real world: visionary and passionate entrepreneurs like Burt Rutan, Richard Branson, Elon Musk, Robert Bigelow, are making a difference. SpaceX cheap access to orbit and asteroid mining being explored Planetary Resources, to name just two.

The region where SRI decided to create our physical headquarter, Boulder Colorado, is an area where the new space industry is growing up, with hundreds of old and new companies.

On May 31 2012, SpaceX successfully completed the historic mission that made Dragon the first commercial spacecraft in history to visit the International Space Station. Previously only four governments — the United States, Russia, Japan and the European Space Agency — had achieved this challenging technical feat.

Average cost of a Dragon/Falcon 9 mission: 133 million. Compared to the shuttle cost (500 million), and the European ATV cost (600 million), it is a reduction of the cost to orbit around 4 times[9]. And the goal announced by Elon Musk is less than 3000 USD / Kg.

China just flown the first woman to the Chinese Space Station, and plans to orbit a bigger manned space station within 2020. More important, Chinese expenditure i n space is double its military expenditure. China clearly considers expansion into space as part of the social development process, something that the western governments seem to be light years away from. We should not be happy, since the Chinese government is the same that is destroying Tibetan culture, but its space policy should be taken as a sample by the western governments.

On another layer the X-37B-OTV-2 (NASA's unmanned Orbital Test Vehicle), reentered few days ago after 469 days in orbit, and landed automatically. The military seem to keep clear in mind the strategic relevance of space, and the high importance, in the future, of orbital vehicles capable of manouvring very much better than the current machines.

However, civilization in general is demonstrating its quite primitive status of awareness of the seriousity of the current situation, and the huge risk of an unrecoverable shift back in history.

Though nobody gives to it the proper relevance (except the small patrol of the astronautic humanists), a kind of space race is ongoing, and nobody – at least in the western world – is concentrating the proper amount of public and private money in it.

The themes of space tourism and commercial space flight are now discussed very much more, in a number of places where they were taboo only a few years ago. For example, I remember in 2006 I was participating in a presentation of a UAV experiment at CIRA (a branch of

Italian Space Agency). I made a quick intervention talking about SpaceShipOne and the low cost access to orbit, and it was a kind of scandal! Nowadays they are inviting us to hold speeches about space tourism at their events.

Our strategy, sketched in our Issue I paper, and coming from our perception of the world, can be largely confirmed. Our perceived world is the Solar System, and it extends to the surrounding Oort Cloud, made of trillions of comets, providing water and basic components of life in the whole Solar System, while Asteroids contain almost pure metals and other minerals. Exo-water means exo-oxygen, and everything needed to support human life and other Earthling forms of life that will accompany us in our expansion.

Our strategy, in the current critical age, must be focused to ignite the human exo-development:

- sharply reduce the cost of reaching orbit (key to everything following)
- focus on Civilian Astronautics
- protect and develop Earth's orbits, which are our interfaces to Cosmos
- master the orbital environment, that will be our greater home, for much of this century
- progressively use exo-resources, from Moon and NEA, to develop the Earth-Moon infrastructure
- use part of the orbiting Space Debris to build the Orbital Infrastructure
- develop SBSP research and demonstrators to feed space customers, in closed sinergy with Civilian Astronautics (SBSP should boost astronautics, and not to create some new thousands tonns of space debris)
- move more public money from military to civilian space activities
- support the shift of investments into the new space industry.

Our four years political agenda (now three years), for bootstrapping a true exo-development maintain its entire validity:

a) cutting the cost to orbit, suborbital and orbital space tourism, industrial development of the Moon and the Near Earth Asteroids; space based solar power
b) stimulate the growth of a new mass space industry - choosing a few suppliers was the old (agencies') method; we must now stimulate the growth of a new mass space industry, oriented to the market (no longer to agencies)
c) International Space Investment Funds
d) tax discounts and friendly financing for the emerging space industry
e) wide international cooperation, for a peaceful space development.

One year after the first SRI congress, a due balance of our action

If our analysis was confirmed, and there is even more evidence that the solution we proposed is the sole solution, we cannot be so proud about what we have achieved – or we could better say what we haven't achieved – in the past year.

Btw, June 2012 was a milestone, foreseen by our four years agenda[10], for checking the status of the SRI Projects. Our 2011 – 2015 agenda was the following one:

- July 2011 - SRI Projects kick-off, 2011 registration campaign kick-off
- January 2012 - Media advertising campaign, Incorporating the SRI US chapter
- June 2012 - SRI Projects check, 2012 registration campaign kick-off
- January 2013 - Media advertising campaign, with first data issued by the SRI Projects
- June 2013 - SRI Projects results evaluation, dissemination and decision about follow ups
- January 2014 - SRI Projects issues dissemination, development of children's projects
- June 2014 - "Medici Space Foundation" building first steps
- January 2015 - "Medici Space Foundation" project check

- June 2015 - SRI second congress, "Medici Space Foundation" incorporation

We have to acknowledge that the main goals of the passed year were not achieved.

The registration campaign never started. The media advertising campaign never taked off either. We just started few weeks ago to re-take the path of the SRI US Chapter incorporation.

We completely failed the public action about some key themes, e.g.: "space debris, human life and health protection against hard radiation in space and low/zero gravity, astrobiology in general, exo-agricolture and exo-farming, Near Earth Asteroids capture and mining"[11]

More in general, we were rather absent from the public scene, and we largely failed, so far, to fight the misinformation and the false metaphysics in the real society. Our political initiative was near zero.

Our tasks, revised

We identify the main problem of the globalized society to be the huge lack of awareness about the risk of implosion of the civilization and about the only possible solution, expansion outside our mother planet.

The main guidelines of the SRI action, during the three years remaining before the 2nd congress, are therefore the following ones:

a) To increase awareness of the need for a space renaissance in society
b) To help the development of the civilian astronautic industry and markets
c) To raise the hope of the people, in the huge possibility to exit the crisis, and retake a path of social growth.

It is our duty to translate the above guidelines in concrete programs and agendas.

In our 2011-2015 program we considered the "Medici Space Foundation" as the last step, to be initiated after SRI had achieved a good public visibility and reputation.

Our three projects (CRAM, BSID and VOSS) were intended as means, to reach the needed visibility.

One year after those decisions, the situation sees two never started projects, and the VOSS project initiated, but:

(i) its propriety is claimed by another entity, thus we cannot consider it a SRI project

(ii) its methodology and goals are not the ones decided by the SRI Congress.

Time is of major importance, and we can no longer consider a two-steps-strategy -- first get visibility, then do concrete work – though the three projects decided by the SRI Congress were however, and still are, worth developing.

We shall start immediately to make the real work, to help the development of the civilian astronautic industry and market.

Our political setup, to unify effort, both public and private, keeps on being the best possible strategy: channeling private and public investment on the *baby* new space industry.

Considering our still few volunteer resources, and the extreme urgency of our tasks, we propose the following essential agenda.

1) **Policy**
   a. create a team of economist and financial experts, with the goal to design the Space Investment Fund
   b. draft a proposal to all the new space entrepreneurs and commercial dealers, to associate in a consortium and subscribe letters of intent, like the following:
   "when the fund will be created, with proper trusted warranties, I will subscribe xxx USD to contribute to the seed capital"
   c. define few essential key and easy concepts, to support the campaign (some were proposed by Patrick some months ago):
      i. *Safe, low-cost space travel is necessary for a peaceful and prosperous future.*
      ii. *The western way of life can be preserved only expanding into space.*
      iii. *Safe, low-cost space travel is necessary also to provide unlimited opportunities for employment, while preserving Earth's natural environment.*

   iv. Humans are using more and more the resources of planet Earth, it was calculated that our civilization would need 1,5 planet Earth or more[12]: so we must soon start to use the unlimited resources of our Solar System, or the damage to Earth's environment, and fighting over Earth's resources, will destroy civilization.
   v. In order to use space resources we need safe, low-cost space travel.
  d. move the proposal to all the potentially interested partners (part of the campaign to launch the new SRI US Chapter)

2) **Campaign.** Concentrate our efforts on the following goals:
  a. create the SRI US Chapter
  b. a SRI US Chapter **launch event**, within 2012, in Boulder Colorado
  c. create the new SRI website, with a blog
  d. run the 2012 membership registration campaign
  e. create a Space Renaissance International voice on Wikipedia (Gail is already working on this).

3) **Projects.** Development of SRI projects and/or participation to other projects shall be carefully traded-off, and decided only in case we have the needed minimal resources, i.e. a project manager and a minimal team (2 or 3 persons).
    a. **CRAM** - Provided that the above conditions exist, priority will be given to the CRAM (Civilization Risk Assessment and Management), with the following set-up:
        i. **Alliances**: Lifeboat Foundation (having a huge discussion in their forum about threats to civilization), and maybe KSU, who could hold also an academic interest in it; also note that KSU is launching a Space Philosophy discussion forum, something that could somehow merge with the SRI philosophic chapter, and maybe constitue the seed of the Space Renaissance Academy (see the SR Manifesto).
        ii. **Methodology**: requirements of the project shall be captured, and a draft statement of works to be done; such a document will be proposed to universities and research entities, to build a working team for the development of the project; money will be collected among sponsors, in order to give birth to prizes for university students
        iii. **SRI goals**: create a scientific evaluation of the global civilization risk, especially if we remain confined within the planetary limits; expand SRI's philosophy and influence in the academic world; get meaningful and prestigious support in the academic world.
    b. **VOSS** – See the dedicated resolution about the SRI participation to the VOSS (Virtual Orbital Space Settlement) project.

TABLE OF CONTENTS

CHAPTER I THE ISSUES PRESENTED TO THE CONGRESS 3
PREMISES..3
ISSUE I – OUR PHILOSOPHICAL UNDERSTANDING OF THE STATUS OF CIVILIZATION AND THE SRI POLITICAL PROGRAM 2011 – 2015..4
    History of the Space Renaissance International..4
    Strategy for space industrialization 4
    Refocusing our commitment to astronautics, i.e. human space flight.......6
    The status of civilization 10
    The main general needs 12
    The program to ignite the Space Renaissance 16
    The SRI agenda from 2011 to 2015 18
    A growth setup for Space Renaissance International 19
ISSUE II – THREE PROJECTS FOR THE SPACE RENAISSANCE 20
    General setup...20
    Projects 21
CHAPTER II THE DISCUSSION 26
    DAY 1 – JUNE 25TH 2011..26
    DAY 2 – JUNE 26TH 2011 47
    DAY 3 – JULY 9TH 2011 74
    DAY 4 – JULY 10TH 2011..94
CHAPTER III THE FINAL RESOLUTION 113
SUMMARIZING THE ACHIEVEMENTS OF THE SRI FIRST CONGRESS..113
POLITICAL GUIDELINES EMERGING FROM THE CONGRESS, FOR OUR PUBLIC OUTREACH VIRAL CAMPAIGN 115
    Fighting Misinformation, toward Exo-Development............................115
    Raising public attention on some disciplines essential for Space Development 118
    Heralding a new breeze of innovation in the political / ideological environment... 120
    Is this the end or the beginning of the space age?...............................121
THE THREE PROJECTS, TO BALANCE OUR COMMUNICATION127
CHAPTER IV 2012 - THE FINAL RESOLUTION UPGRADE 128
CIVILIZATION STATUS – AN UPGRADE 128
    Our analysis keeps entirely its validity 128
    A necessary actualization about energy and raw materials 131
    Human impact on biosphere and the risk of civilization implosion 133
    However, a kind of space race is under way.. 135
ONE YEAR AFTER THE FIRST SRI CONGRESS, A DUE BALANCE OF OUR ACTION.. 138
OUR TASKS, REVISED 139
REFERENCES.. 144

References

1. "Three Theses for the Space Renaissance", A. V. Autino, P. Q. Collins, A. Cavallo – 2011, lulu.com - http://www.lulu.com/commerce/index.php?fBuyContent=10003567
2. http://www.spacerenaissance.org/SRIC/SRIC-HOME.html
3. http://www.nss.org/resources/library/videos/GreasonISDC2011.pdf
4. http://orbitaldebris.jsc.nasa.gov/faqs.html
5. http://en.wikipedia.org/wiki/Kondratiev_wave
6. http://news.bbc.co.uk/2/hi/science/nature/2381559.stm
7. http://www.fao.org/docrep/016/i2727e/i2727e00.htm
8. http://www.spacefuture.com/archive/why_implementing_the_space_option_is_necessary_for_society.shtml
9. http://en.wikipedia.org/wiki/Comparison_of_orbital_launch_systems
10. http://www.spacerenaissance.org/SRIC/SRIC_ISSUE_I_the_SRI_program_2011_2015.pdf
11. http://www.spacerenaissance.org/SRIC/SRIC_Final_Resolution.pdf
12. http://www.footprintnetwork.org/en/index.php/gfn/page/world_footprint/
13. http://www.economist.com/node/18897425

www.ingramcontent.com/pod-product-compliance
Lightning Source LLC
Chambersburg PA
CBHW060859170526
45158CB00001B/416